PHYSICIAN MANAGERS AND THE LAW

Employment and Personal Service Contracts

American Academy of Medical Directors

American College of Physician Executives

Physician Executive Management Center

One Urban Centre
4830 W. Kennedy Blvd., Suite 648
Tampa, Florida 33609-2517
(813) 873-2000
As of January 1, 1988: (813) 287-2000

"This publication is designed to provide accurate and authoritative information in regard to the subject matter covered. It is sold with the understanding that the publisher is not engaged in rendering legal, accounting, or other professional service. If legal advice or other expert assistance is required, the services of a competent professional should be sought." *From a Declaration of Principles jointly adopted by a committee of the American Bar Association and a Committee of Publishers.*

ISBN: 0-9605218-4-4

Printed in the United States of America
by Lithocolor Printing Corp., Tampa, Florida.

Foreword

This monograph was produced by the American Academy of Medical Directors to respond to the expressed informational needs of physician executives. In the fall of 1986, at the Academy's National Institute on Health Care Leadership and Management, several members of the Academy were asked to participate in a focus group to determine the topics of major interest to physician executives. Legal issues were of prime concern, with an emphasis on contract law. Two areas of contract law were mentioned repeatedly-- employment and personal services and joint ventures.

With this monograph, the Academy addresses one of those areas of concern-- employment and personal services contracts. In designing the monograph, we decided that, beyond a general description of such contract law, the application of contract law in various health care settings should, if at all possible, be discussed by physician executives who also have an understanding of the law. In that regard, the Academy is fortunate. Three members were identified who had combined medical and legal education. More important, they come from various health care environments and were enthusiastic about participating in this project. Drs. James B. Couch, MD, JD, Dale H. Cowan, MD, JD, and Bernard T. Ferrari, MD, JD, are joined in this publishing venture by Douglas A. Hastings, Esq., and Joseph E. Lynch, Esq., of the Washington, DC, law firm Epstein Becker Borsody & Green. In addition, Gail B. Agrawal, Esq., was enlisted by Dr. Ferrari to coauthor the chapter on employment and personal services contracts in group practices.

Physician executives, like other managers in the health care field, are called upon to understand and deal with a number of disciplines that are alien to their basic education and training. The law is such a discipline. While it is not necessary for the nonattorney to deal with the issues of law in detail, the wary manager will desire at least a skeletal background in those issues. If this monograph provides that background, it will have fulfilled the Academy's goals in this publishing endeavor.

Roger S. Schenke
Executive Vice President
American Academy of Medical Directors
Tampa, Florida
October 1987

Introduction

Roger Schenke, Academy Executive Vice President, advises in this monograph's foreword that every health care executive needs to know "at least a little bit about a lot of things." As the uncertainties and complexities of medical management increase, so too does the list of "things." Finance, marketing, personnel management, organization theory, product line management, and cost accounting are part of the successful manager's armamentarium. So too must be the law.

The breadth and depth of disciplines needed by the successful organization are great; the practicality of a single medical manager becoming expert in any of them is small. The intricacies and specialties of law compound the difficulty. A goal for the executive, therefore, is to know enough to be able to judge the quality of the expertise and advice required from others.

Assisting with this goal is the objective of this new Academy publication. Its aim is to introduce the reader to some of the certainties and vagaries of employment and personal services contracts. The authors explain what should be and what should not be part of such contracts in each of four health care environments: hospitals, HMOs, PPOs, and group practices. We believe the monograph will be helpful in judging the quality of the contracts and the advice you may seek in these situations.

Robert B. Klint, MD, MHA
President
American Academy of Medical Directors
Tampa, Florida
October 1987

Contents

Chapter 1

PHYSICIAN SERVICES CONTRACTS

Douglas A. Hastings, Esq., and Joseph E. Lynch, Esq.

Douglas A. Hastings and Joseph E. Lynch are attorneys with the Washington, D.C., law firm Epstein Becker Borsody & Green, P.C. The firm specializes in the practice of law in health care settings.

Mr. Hastings' clients include hospital systems and alliances, individual hospitals, physician groups, health maintenance organizations, preferred provider organizations, insurance companies, peer review organizations, and other health entities. His areas of legal expertise include corporate law, tax law, securities law, administrative/regulatory law, and contract law. He has worked closely with various insurance companies, hospitals, and physician groups in establishing joint ventures, particularly in the alternative delivery systems area. Mr. Hastings serves as a Visiting Lecturer at the Duke University Department of Health Administration and speaks and publishes regularly on topics related to health care law in general and alternative delivery systems in particular.

Mr. Lynch's legal practice focuses on the corporate and regulatory aspects of alternative health care delivery. In addition, he has a legislative/lobbying practice concentrated on federal and state health care legislation affecting hospitals. Prior to joining Epstein Becker Borsody & Green, P.C., he served as a judicial law clerk for the Federal District Court in Charlottesville, Virginia.

It is rare in the modern health care setting that a transaction takes place without a contract between two or more parties. For better or worse, contract law is a central element in the increasingly complex health care environment. Contracts determine the basic rights and obligations among the parties involved in virtually every significant health care arrangement or delivery system.

Important categories of contracts commonly used in health care settings today include, for example, provider (i.e., hospital and physician) services agreements, employment agreements, joint purchasing agreements, third-party insurer or payer agreements, management agreements, stock purchase agreements, shareholder agreements, and joint venture or partnership agreements. In addition, contracts are essential to the operation of the newer forms of health care delivery or financing, such as health maintenance organizations (HMOs), preferred provider arrangements (PPAs), and ambulatory care centers and clinics. Indeed, many PPAs are nothing more than a series of contracts linking payers, employers, providers, beneficiaries, and possibly management or administrative service companies.

For physicians engaged in health care management, an area of particular interest within the general umbrella of health care contracting is physician services contracts. Physicians' services are essential to any health care delivery system or organization. Consequently, the legal documents setting forth the rights, obligations, and expectations of both the physicians and the systems or organizations are of primary importance. If such legal documents are ambiguous, underinclusive, legally unenforceable, or otherwise deficient, the result may be significant added expense and embarrassment to the physicians and the systems or organizations, as well as inconvenience to patients.

The purpose of this monograph is to provide physicians involved in health care management with a broad-based perspective on physician contracting as well as specific information designed to help avoid the pitfalls of deficient contract planning and drafting. As the following chapters illustrate, most lawsuits over contract interpretation can be avoided through careful contract planning and drafting.

This overview chapter is intended to provide a general introduction to contract law, emphasizing the fundamental elements of a valid contract. Later chapters will address the application of contract law in specific health care settings.

Employees and Independent Contractors

Before we discuss basic contract principles, a brief word is in order regarding the difference between employees and independent contractors. Most physician services agreements create an independent contractor relationship between the physician and the other party to the agreement. Conversely, most contracts for employment of a hospital-based physician or of a chief executive officer of a hospital, HMO, clinic, or other health care company create an employer/employee relationship between the parties to the contract.

In very basic terms, an independent contractor agrees to perform work according to the individual's own skills and judgment and is not subject to the direct supervision of the other party to the agreement. By contrast, an employee is, in theory, not permitted to exercise discretion in providing services, is more closely supervised, and at all times is under the control and direction of the employer. Obviously, the question of whether an individual is an independent contractor or an employee may sometimes be unclear, especially in connection with highly skilled and highly educated practitioners such as physicians.

Both employment agreements and independent contractor agreements are subject to the basic principles of contract law discussed below. Both types of contracts involve a description of rights and obligations concerning payment arrangements, termination provisions, and similar key elements. However, the employee/independent contractor distinction is important because of the additional regulatory oversight that exists under federal and state law for employer-employee relationships. Typically, such laws do not apply to independent contractor arrangements. A partial list of legislation creating employer obligations to employees includes federal income tax withholding requirements, unemployment compensation laws, labor relations and employment laws, and antidiscrimination laws.

A detailed analysis of the case law dealing with employment versus independent contractor relationships is beyond the scope of this monograph. Any organization contemplating a contract with a physician should consider whether the desired arrangement may create an employer/employee relationship. If so, the organization must adhere to the additional requirements applicable to employer-employee relationships.

General Contract Principles

The general principles of contract law deal with the factors necessary to form a binding contract and with the means for enforcing a contract or pursuing other remedies in the event of a contract breach. The following discussion of those principles is necessarily general, because the facts of each case are unique. Negotiation and preparation of actual contracts should include consultation with experienced counsel familiar with the facts. Also, all contracts are substantially governed by state law, and physician services contracts are often governed by federal law. Consequently, matters concerning formation, performance, breach, and enforcement of a particular health care services contract must be examined in light of applicable state and federal laws and regulations.

Contract Formation

A contract is a legally enforceable agreement between two or more parties that specifies the obligations to which each party is bound. The central distinction between a contract and a gratuitous promise is that the latter involves a statement or agreement that is not legally enforceable.

Generally, there are five factors necessary to make an agreement a legally enforceable contract:

- Mutual assent

- Definite provisions

- Exchange of obligations

- Legal capacity

- Legal purpose

It is important to note that although virtually all physician services contracts are reduced to writing, in most cases an oral agreement including the above five factors is just as binding and enforceable as a written agreement to the same effect.

Mutual Assent. Mutual assent means that each party to a contract understands and agrees to all the provisions of the contract. Mutual assent is often referred to as a "meeting of the minds." The parties to an agreement do not have a meeting of the minds unless (1) each party understands and agrees to the same contract provisions and (2) all parties' understanding of those provisions is the same.

For instance, there is no meeting of the minds in the following examples involving a medical services agreement between a physician and an HMO:

1. The physician agrees to a compensation arrangement that cannot be changed without the physician's consent. However, the HMO agrees to a compensation arrangement that can be changed by the HMO without the physician's consent. In this case there is no meeting of the minds, because the parties have not agreed to the same contract terms.

2. The agreement requires the physician to provide all "Physician Services" to HMO enrollees, but does not define what services are included in the term "Physician Services." The physician understands the term to include all office procedures except surgical procedures. Conversely, the HMO understands the term to include all office procedures, including surgical procedures. There is no meeting of the minds in this case, because the parties did not have the same understanding of the contract term "Physician Services."

Typically, mutual assent is demonstrated by each party's formally accepting, or executing, the agreement. Generally, the execution of a contract is preceded by a negotiation process involving the review and revision of a proposed contract drafted by one of the parties.

A proposed contract including the remaining four factors discussed in this section constitutes an offer of a contract. The party submitting a proposed contract is known as the offeror, and the party to whom a proposed contract is given is known as the offeree.

Any offeree can make a proposed contract into an enforceable contract with the offeror by agreeing to all its provisions. However, if the offeree makes any changes to the proposed contract, those changes, along with the unchanged provisions, become a new proposed contract, or counteroffer. A counteroffer constitutes a rejection of the original proposed contract. By making a counteroffer, a party relinquishes the right to make the original proposed contract into an enforceable contract, unless the offeror submits the original proposed contract again.

In a negotiation process that culminates in an executed agreement, the offers and counteroffers eventually produce provisions to which the parties assent. By accepting the final version of those provisions, the parties acknowledge their mutual assent. If the agreement contains the remaining four factors discussed below, the parties have entered into an enforceable contract.

Definite Provisions. A corollary to mutual assent is the requirement that the provisions agreed to by the parties must be specific enough to be enforced by a court or other authorized third party, such as an arbiter. Without such specificity, it is impossible to determine the obligations each party has agreed to undertake.

In the second example above, the term "Physician Services," standing alone, is too indefinite, because a court or arbiter cannot determine which procedures the physician has agreed to perform. Thus, the physician services agreement in the second example above is not a contract, because one of its key provisions is too indefinite to be enforced.

Even if an agreement has a seemingly indefinite provision, it still may constitute an enforceable contract if the agreement shows that the parties intended the provision in question to have a definite meaning. For instance, the term "Physician Services" in the above example could be sufficiently definite if:

■ The parties include in their agreement a definition of the term "Physician Services" that specifies the procedures a physician must agree to perform.

■ The parties define the term "Physician Services" in their agreement by referencing a list of procedures in another document (such as a physician reference guide).

■ The parties define the term "Physician Services" in their agreement by referencing a standard meaning of the term that is commonly accepted.

In short, each provision of an agreement must have a definite meaning, as specified either in the agreement itself or by reference to a definition or other standard outside the agreement. If any provision is so indefinite that it is subject to more than one interpretation, the agreement will not constitute an enforceable contract.

Exchange of Obligations. An agreement generally is not an enforceable contract unless it includes an exchange of obligations by the parties. Each party must undertake specified obligations in exchange for the obligations undertaken by every other party to the agreement. The exchange of obligations is often referred to as the "consideration" for the contract.

In a typical physician services contract, the consideration is the physician's agreement to perform specified services in exchange for the other party's agreement to pay specified compensation to the physician. Thus, the obligations undertaken by each party serve as the inducement for the other party to enter into the contract.

In the absence of an exchange of obligations, a proposed agreement usually constitutes a nonenforceable promise. For example, unless a physician undertakes some obligation in return for an HMO's promise to make the physician a participating provider, the physican generally cannot enforce the HMO's promise. Because there is no exchange of obligations in such a case, the HMO's promise is merely gratuitous. As a general rule, a gratuitous promise lacks consideration and therefore is not an enforceable contract.

One exception to the general rule involves cases in which one party makes a gratuitous promise and the other party relies on the promise. For instance, if the physician in the above example relied on the HMO's promise by dropping a clinical practice and moving across the country to settle in the HMO's service area, the physician might be able to enforce the HMO's promise to make the physician a participating provider.

If a court determines that the physician in the above case acted reasonably in relying on the HMO's promise, the court is likely to conclude that an enforceable contract existed (provided that the HMO's promise contained terms that were sufficiently definite to be enforced by the court). In such a case, the physician's reasonable reliance serves as, or replaces, the consideration for the contract.

Legal Capacity. The requirement of legal capacity means that the parties to an agreement must be legally capable of entering into a binding contract. Generally, a party has legal capacity if applicable state law recognizes the party as being responsible for its own actions.

For example, many states do not recognize or enforce agreements entered into by an individual younger than a certain age. Similarly, states may not recognize or enforce agreements entered into by individuals who have been legally determined to be mentally incapacitated. Consequently, agreements entered into by minors and other individuals without legal capacity may not be enforced.

Legal Purpose. Even if an agreement contains all of the foregoing factors, it may still not constitute a binding contract if the agreement is designed to accomplish an objective that is not legal. The question of whether an agreement's purpose is legal may depend on both state and federal law. If the agreement's purpose is not legal under applicable law, the agreement will not be enforceable.

Breach of Contract

An agreement including each of the five factors discussed above constitutes an enforceable contract. Parties entering into an enforceable contract generally must perform all their obligations as specified in the contract, unless those obligations are (1) modified pursuant to an amendment procedure established in the contract, (2) modified by mutual consent of the parties, or (3) excused because of circumstances that the parties did not foresee when they entered into the contract. For example, if a surgeon loses hand motor control, the surgeon's failure to honor obligations under a physician services contract may be excused. The question of whether a party's failure to perform will be excused depends on the facts of each case.

Failure of a party to perform contractual obligations generally constitutes a breach of the contract. When faced with a breach of contract, a nonbreaching party can pursue several courses of action, as discussed below.

Remedies for Breach of Contract

If a party breaches a contract, the nonbreaching party should consult the contract to determine whether it includes any provisions specifying actions that must be taken in the event of a breach. For example, a contract may specify that the nonbreaching party must notify the breaching party of the breach and request that it be cured within a specified period. Even if a contract does not contain such a "notice and cure" provision, it often is advisable, prior to pursuing other remedies, for the nonbreaching party to provide the breaching party with such notice and with an opportunity to cure the breach.

If the contract has no provisions on breach, or the breach is not cured after the nonbreaching party complies with the contract provisions regarding breaches, the nonbreaching party generally may pursue one or both of the following courses of action:

■ Terminate the contract.

■ Sue to recover monetary losses and expenses resulting from the breach.

Decisions regarding whether a breach has occurred and which remedy or remedies to pursue in the event of a breach should be based on advice of counsel familiar with the facts of the case.

A remedy for breach that typically is not available in a case involving a physician services contract is a lawsuit to enforce the terms of the contract. Such a lawsuit often is referred to as a lawsuit seeking "specific performance."

Specific performance usually is not available as a remedy for breach of a physician services contract, because the courts typically will not specifically enforce a contract involving an ongoing relationship in which one party must perform personal services to the satisfaction of the other party.

In addition, specific performance is only available in cases where no monetary payment by the breaching party would be sufficient to compensate the nonbreaching party. Because a monetary payment is likely to be adequate compensation for the breach of a physician services contract, specific performance typically is not available as a remedy in such a case.

Terminate the Contract. As a general rule, when a party breaches a contract, the nonbreaching party is under no duty to continue performing obligations under the contract. The nonbreaching party usually cannot terminate the contract on the basis of a minor breach, such as a brief delay in payment, that does not substantially affect the nonbreaching party's rights under the contract. Nevertheless, the nonbreaching party may still sue to recover losses and expenses resulting from the minor breach. Determining whether a breach is major or minor turns on the facts of each case.

In some cases, the nonbreaching party may be willing to hold the contract in abeyance until the breaching party cures the breach. For example, if a physician is not complying with the specialist referral procedures specified in an HMO physician services contract, the HMO may choose not to terminate the contract but merely to withhold performance of its obligations under the contract until the physician complies.

In other cases, the nonbreaching party may determine that the contract must be terminated immediately to minimize harm resulting from the breach. For instance, if the above example also involved the physician's failure to comply with hospital admission procedures specified in the contract, the HMO might decide that the unwarranted overutilization of services resulting from the physician's actions requires immediate termination of the contract.

If the nonbreaching party decides to terminate the contract, it should immediately notify the breaching party. Such a notice guards against ambiguity concerning whether the contract is still in force.

Sue to Recover Monetary Losses and Expenses Resulting from the Breach. The nonbreaching party may initiate a lawsuit seeking monetary recovery from the breaching party for reasonable losses and expenses. Such a recovery typically is referred to as "compensatory damages."

In the typical breach of contract case, there is no recovery for "pain and suffering." However, in a case involving a particularly egregious breach of contract, the nonbreaching party may be able to sue successfully for punitive damages. The question of whether punitive damages may be awarded in a breach of contract case depends on applicable state law and the facts of the case.

To recover compensatory damages for a breach of contract, the nonbreaching party must demonstrate that:

■ The parties had entered into an enforceable contract (i.e., an agreement containing the five factors mentioned in the previous section).

- An unexcused breach of the contract has occurred because of the actions or omissions of the breaching party.

- As a result of the breach, the nonbreaching party has suffered monetary losses.

- The nonbreaching party is willing and able to perform its obligations under the contract.

In proving damages resulting from a breach, the nonbreaching party often must show that, after the breach occurred, the nonbreaching party took all steps necessary to minimize losses. Typically, the nonbreaching party is not permitted to recover compensatory damages for losses or expenses that the nonbreaching party could reasonably have prevented after the breach.

If the nonbreaching party can demonstrate that the above elements exist in the case, the court is likely to rule that the breaching party must pay compensatory damages.

Generally, the court or jury determines the amount of compensation on the basis of all evidence presented concerning the damages resulting from the breach. However, if the parties' contract specifies the amount of compensatory damages to be paid in the event of a breach, the court typically rules that the specified amount must be paid.

A contract provision specifying the compensatory damages to be paid if a breach occurs often is referred to as a "liquidated damages" provision. Parties generally include a liquidated damages provision in their contract if they believe it will be difficult or impossible to calculate the monetary losses that would result if a breach occurs. Generally, courts will enforce such a liquidated damages provision unless the amount of the liquidated damages is substantially greater than the nonbreaching party's actual losses and expenses.

Chapter 2

EMPLOYMENT CONTRACTS

IN GROUP PRACTICES

Bernard T. Ferrari, M.D., J.D.
Gail B. Agrawal, Esq.

Bernard T. Ferrari, MD, JD, received his undergraduate and medical degrees from the University of Rochester. After completing his general surgery residency at the University of California, Los Angeles, and a colon and rectal surgery fellowship at the Alton Ochsner Medical Foundation, he joined the Ochsner Clinic as a colon and rectal surgeon. He also received a juris doctor degree magna cum laude from Loyola University in New Orleans, where he was a member of the Law Review, and a master of business administration from Tulane University, where he was elected to Beta Gamma Sigma. He currently holds the position of Assistant Medical Director at the Ochsner Clinic, New Orleans, with responsibility for business operations and legal affairs. Dr. Ferrari is a member of Phi Beta Kappa and Alpha Omega Alpha and has contributed to the medical, legal, and management literatures.

Gail Agrawal, JD, MPH, received a master of public health degree in health systems management from Tulane School of Public Health and Tropical Medicine, where she was elected to Delta Omega. She was awarded the juris doctor degree summa cum laude from Tulane Law School, where she was an editor of the Tulane Law Review and was elected to the Order of the Coif. After completing law school, Ms. Agrawal served as a law clerk to the Honorable John Minor Wisdom, Senior Judge, United States Court of Appeals for the Fifth Circuit, and the Honorable Sandra Day O'Connor, Associate Justice, Supreme Court of the United States. She is currently employed by Monroe & Lemann in New Orleans.

Physicians more frequently than ever before are entering into contracts that define how they will exercise their professional skills in relationship with one another. A contract or an agreement simply expresses the reciprocal legal obligations to which two or more parties commit themselves. Physicians are very familiar with the concept of an obligation, for it is the physician's obligation to the patient that forms the nucleus of medical practice.

One of the major ingredients of an obligation, and the ingredient that is most familiar to physicians, is duty, which, in its simplest terms, defines what each party will do for the other. A legal obligation has the added dimension of the legal bond, which defines the link between the parties entering into the agreement and permits recourse against the party failing in its duty.

This chapter will concentrate on employment agreements, which share a generic structure with other legal agreements. The chapter will follow the basic outline of Chapter 1, highlighting the special factors that deserve consideration in employment agreements.

A physician learns early in his medical education that the technical aspects of medicine, although very engaging for the student, once mastered, become second nature to most physicians. On the other hand, most experienced physicians will agree that it is the conceptual scientific underpinnings of medical practice that provide physicians throughout their careers with the ability to continue to understand and cope with disease processes in light of the emergence of new knowledge and the acquisition of experience.

This same reasoning can be applied to legal education. Although learning how to draft a legal document utilizing the appropriate legal lexicon is a skill that might be sought by a law student, or in this situation a physician manager, it is the legal conceptual architecture that will provide the basic understanding and substance of the legal agreement.

Moreover, this conceptual architecture can be of great assistance in negotiations, for it provides a mental checklist as one proceeds through the negotiation process.

Even the most experienced physician manager will likely need competent legal counsel to draft agreements that reflect the intent and the binding commitment of the parties. Furthermore, because different states impose different laws on employment agreements, competent legal counsel in a particular jurisdiction is essential, especially when agreements reach across state lines. To eliminate disputes over which state's law applies, the agreement should contain a choice-of-law clause identifying the governing law.

Definition of a Contract

Not every agreement is a contract, and not every contract is legally enforceable. Although a completely satisfactory definition for the term has never been devised, a contract may be characterized generally as a promise, or set of promises, to which two or more parties agree and which will be enforced by a court of competent jurisdiction. In the case of an employment contract, the potential employer promises to employ the candidate, the physician, for a certain amount of compensation and benefits in exchange for the physician- employee's promise to perform certain specified services.

Before any contract can be formed, an offer must be made. The law defines an offer as a promise to do, or to refrain from doing, some specified act in the future. The making of an offer creates a power of acceptance in the

---

recipient. In the case of an employment contract, the employer promises to employ the physician at a specified sum. By accepting the offer, the physician transforms the promise of employment into a contractual obligation.

The physician may accept the offer by his conduct, for example by appearing for work and beginning to perform services, or by his words. If the offer is in writing, it can be accepted by signing the writing, even if the person accepting fails to read the terms. The employer would be permitted to rely on the physician's written assent to what he knew or should have known was an offer of employment. If the physician purports to accept the offer of employment, but attempts to add terms or conditions not contained in the original offer, his "acceptance" is deemed a counteroffer, rather than an acceptance of the original offer. The potential employer would then have the power of acceptance of the counteroffer, and his original offer would be deemed revoked.

The physician may accept the offer only as long as it is outstanding. An offer may be revoked by the lapse of a specified time or, if no time is specified, by the passage of a reasonable time. The offer may also be revoked by certain events, if they are specified in the terms of the offer.

Furthermore, the physician may accept only what is offered by the potential employer. In this regard, one must distinguish "offers" from predictions of preliminary negotiations. Suppose the Acme Medical Group, through its administrator, Mr. Able, offers employment to Dr. Bailey. The Group promises to pay Dr. Bailey a specified sum and to provide attendant benefits if he accepts its offer of employment. At the time he extends the offer, Mr. Able tells Dr. Bailey that, if he accepts the Group's offer of employment, he anticipates that in five years Dr. Bailey will be the head of the Group and will earn in excess of $1,000,000 a year. The first statement was an offer of employment, which Dr. Bailey was empowered to accept. Mr. Able's second statement, in contrast, was an expression of opinion or a prophecy, not an offer. Dr. Bailey was not empowered to accept the position as head of the Group at the predicted salary, because it was not offered to him.

The formation of a contract by offer and acceptance requires agreement, or mutual assent, to the same terms. Mutual assent has been characterized as a "meeting of the minds." But a meeting of the minds is more a poetic, than a realistic, assessment of the requirement of mutual assent. The law calls for an objective manifestation, whether oral or by conduct, of agreement between the parties. Suppose Dr. Bailey accepts Acme Medical Group's offer of employment and states that he agrees to devote his full time and energy to the practice of the Group. Secretly, Dr. Bailey has reservations and actually intends to devote some part of his time and effort to a separate practice. If Dr. Bailey is called into court for breach of his agreement to devote his full time and energy to the Group, the court will not be sympathetic to his defense that there was not a true "meeting of the minds" because, despite what Dr. Bailey said, he privately planned to maintain a practice separate from the Group. The court will consider what a reasonable person in the Group's position would conclude from Dr. Bailey's words or actions. In this hypothetical example, the court would probably find that Dr. Bailey had entered into a valid contract, notwithstanding his secret reservations.

When an offer of employment is made and accepted, mutual assent is objectively manifested, and each party is bound to perform certain specified obligations, a contract has been formed. The contract is enforceable in a court of law unless it violates a state or federal statute, is against public policy, or has an illegal purpose. It is not necessary that the contract be in writing, although, as a matter of planning, a written document is preferable.

You will note in the above hypothetical case that Dr. Bailey never received a written agreement setting forth the terms of his employment contract with the Acme Medical Group, but the contract was nonetheless binding and enforceable. The question of whether a contract is formed before, or in the absence of, a written agreement is one of intent. Did the parties intend that a formal writing would be executed before either was bound, or was a writing intended merely as an affirmation of a previously reached agreement? In the former case, an oral agreement is not a binding contract; in the latter, the contract is formed when the oral agreement is reached.

A contract is formed only when the parties agree to the same terms. One of the factors that will be considered in determining whether an oral agreement is intended to be a binding contract is the extent to which the material terms of the agreement are certain and definite. Certainty can be provided in the offer, in the acceptance, or by subsequent conduct. In employment contracts, the issue of indefiniteness is usually raised in the context of duration or term. As a general rule, if no term is stated in an employment contract, most courts will find that employment-at-will was intended, even in circumstances in which the parties have couched the compensation terms on an annual or monthly basis. Some courts, however, have ruled that hiring at a stipulated annual or monthly wage evidences an intent to hire for a definite term. In some jurisdictions, state law limits the length of time to which an individual may commit in an employment contract. If a longer term is specified, the term will not be judicially enforced.

Although many employment contracts are not reduced to writing, written contracts are the norm when dealing with key managerial or professional employees and those who are employed for short periods to perform specific assignments. The principal functions of a written contract are to clarify the terms of employment as much as possible, to provide both the employer and the employee some assurance with respect to their duties and termination rights, and to avoid protracted legal disputes. The drafting of employment contracts presents many opportunities for clarification and for determination of the rights of the parties that are not available in oral agreements.

When an agreement has been reduced to a writing that is a complete and final statement of the parties' agreement, extrinsic evidence, whether oral or otherwise, will not be admitted in a court of law for the purpose of changing or contradicting the agreement. This rule is known as the parol evidence rule. Three elements must be present before the parol evidence rule will apply. The writing must be final; it must be complete; and it must be a total integration of the terms of the agreement. For example, if the written contract states that the physician-employee will be paid $70,000 a year, the parol evidence rule would exclude the physician's testimony, along with any supporting written documentation, aimed at proving that the agreed-upon figure was $75,000.

The parol evidence rule does not exclude evidence of contemporaneous or prior negotiations or expressions to show that the writing was not intended to be operative or that it was conditional, nor does it apply to evidence that the agreement is void or voidable due to illegality, fraud, mistake, or duress. Evidence would be admissible to show, for example, that the contract setting forth the $70,000 figure was merely a draft, rather than a final statement of the parties' agreement, or that the physician's signature on the agreement was obtained by fraud.

As a practical matter, disputes over whether the parol evidence rule applies can be avoided by a clause providing that the employment contract contains the entire agreement of the parties and supersedes all prior agreements, representations and understandings, whether written or otherwise, between the parties and that there are no representations, warranties, understandings, or agreements other than those expressly set forth in the contract.

Note that the parol evidence rule does not exclude evidence of subsequent agreements or modifications. To avoid disputes over whether an agreement has been modified or amended, the contract should provide expressly that no amendment will be valid or enforceable unless it is reduced to writing and duly signed by all parties.

Parties: Who May Contract

Every contract must be entered into by at least two juridical parties. A juridical party is considered for this discussion as a party that the law recognizes as a discrete legal entity. A legal entity can be an actual living individual or it can be a nonliving entity such as a partnership or a corporation.

If two parties are to contract with each other, they must have the legal capacity to legally bind themselves. The concept of legal capacity usually evokes thoughts of infants and the mentally infirm, neither at first blush being particularly relevant to employment contracts with physicians. However, there is one note of relevance in this area that must be considered when agreements are executed. An intoxicated individual is usually considered mentally infirm under the law for the time that he is intoxicated, although courts are reluctant to invalidate a contract on this ground absent some element of overreaching. For this reason, serious negotiation concerning an employment agreement and certainly the execution of any legal document should be conducted when neither signatory can claim intoxication or any other impairment of his reasoning powers as a defense.

There are other aspects of legal capacity that may not be as apparent as the one mentioned above. When one party enters into an agreement with another, it is important to ascertain whether the individual entering into the agreement has the legal capacity to bind other individuals or an entity that will be performing the duty expressed in the agreement. An example may help clarify this concept. Let us assume that you wish to employ a group of three cardiologists and you have been negotiating with one of the cardiologists who holds himself out to be the "head" of the group. We would find it most important to question whether this individual can bind not only himself, but the other two cardiologists as well. This may depend in part on the legal relationship among the three cardiologists. They may be employees of their own professional corporation or association, partners in a partnership, or three separate cardiologists whose relationship is limited to sharing office space. As a matter of fact, the possible relationships between the three cardiologists are many. If the individual with whom you are conducting negotiations represents the other two cardiologists or the entity to which the cardiologists belong in a legal sense, he may be classified as an agent.

The concept of agency is extremely important in contract law. The broadest definition of a legal agent is one whose actions result in consequences for the one he represents, or the principal, the same as if the principal were taking the actions himself. The powers of an agent can be full--that is, every legal action he takes is binding on the principal--or partial. In the latter circumstance, the agent and the principal have agreed that the agent can legally bind the principal but only within certain restrictions. For example, a physician might enlist another physician as agent only to negotiate a contract within a certain period, after which the agent has no power to legally bind the principal. A physician also might enlist another as agent in negotiations with one potential employer but not with another.

From a bargaining point of view, we have always found it helpful when we enter into negotiations with an individual to define his role. Does he have the authority to bind the entity or individuals for whom he is speaking? Will he have to return to the entity or individual for permission to enter into a legally binding agreement? Who will have to approve his actions before a contract can be legally binding if he cannot execute the contract himself? All too often one may find oneself happily concluding a negotiation when the individual with whom one is negotiating states "Well, now I'll have to go back to my associates and see if they think this is okay." It would be better to avoid what could be not only a legal problem but also a negotiation ploy by defining in the beginning who the parties will be and what their powers are.

If a physician with whom you are negotiating represents a legal entity, such as a corporation or a partnership, there are usually laws in a particular jurisdiction that make clear the manner in which such an agent is empowered and what those powers may be. Under most state corporate laws, there are defined actions that officers or representatives of the corporation can undertake. Some of these actions can be performed by the officer or representative without the approval of a board of directors. However, either under state law or under the articles of incorporation or bylaws of a corporation, there are actions that an officer or representative cannot take without approval by the board of directors. Usually this approval is evidenced by a resolution that recites that the board of directors met as a quorum in a legally assembled meeting and states the specific power that is being given to the officer. If an individual finds himself entering into an agreement with a corporate officer or representative, it behooves him to ascertain whether the officer or representative of the corporation is acting within his legally bestowed powers. In many jurisdictions, a resolution by the board of directors is not needed if the officer has consistently conducted past negotiations with the other contracting party and executed past agreements, holding himself out as the one who could bind the corporation. But it is always better to query the need for a resolution than to find oneself in possession of a defective contract.

When dealing with a partner representing his partnership, the agency issue may be even more complicated, depending on your jurisdiction. Some states may statutorily dictate the power of a partner to enter into an agreement binding his fellow partners, while other states may allow wider discretionary powers, depending in large part on the partnership agreement.

To clarify this issue, consider the hypothetical situation of employing the Acme Cardiology Group, a partnership under the laws of your state that has as its partners Drs. Smith, Jones, and Bailey. Also assume that it is Dr. Smith who provides the major attraction and impetus for you to contract with this group, but that the three physicians in their partnership agreement have previously agreed that any one partner can leave the partnership with 30 days' notice to the other partners. What if Dr. Smith gives notice to his partners that he is leaving the partnership after the partnership has signed an agreement to be employed by your group? Have you contracted with Dr. Smith? Is your contract now with the Acme Cardiology Group and Dr. Smith who has left the group, or is it simply with the Acme Cardiology Group, with Dr. Smith no longer legally bound to the contract?

To take the safe course, we recommend that you have all partners execute the agreement, thus binding them as individuals and as an entity. This will avoid the pitfall that the hypothetical case of Acme Cardiology Group illustrates. Perhaps the most effective way to ensure that the party with whom one has contracted was legally empowered to execute the agreement is to include language in the contract so warranting. For example, when entering into an agreement with a corporate entity, we include a clause that provides that the contracting party warrants and represents that it is a corporation duly organized, validly existing, and in good standing under the laws of the relevant state; that all corporate actions on the part of the contracting party that are necessary to authorize it to enter into, execute, and perform the contract in accordance with its terms have been taken; and that no consent, approval, or authorization of or by any authority is required as a condition precedent to the valid and lawful execution and performance of the contract. Similar language can be drafted for agreements with partnerships.

A common point of confusion that relates to this same subject is the concept that although one cannot contract with oneself, one can contract with a juridical entity that includes oneself. A partner not only can be a member of that partnership but also can contract with the partnership. In the example above we dealt with a partner leaving the partnership when the partnership was legally bound under an employment agreement. Suppose that you are Dr. Bailey, a partner of the Acme Cardiology Group, negotiating with a large medical group that wishes to employ Acme. To better secure your partner Dr. Smith's legal duty to the partnership, the partnership may want to have an employment contract with Dr. Smith. Therefore, there will be a legally binding contract between Acme and Dr. Smith, thereby completing the legal link. In creating such links, one must remember that the two parties entering into a contract must be juridically separate. Each party must have a separate legal identity but not necessarily a separate personal identity. The difference is subtle, but as we have illustrated, can be very important.

Relationship Between the Parties

The agreement should also define the legal relationship between the involved parties. In the hypothetical contract between your group and the Acme Cardiology Group, the contracting parties probably intend to stand in the relationship of independent contractors. In contrast, the Acme Cardiology Group and its nonpartner physicians stand in the relationship of employer and employee. A third possible relationship is that of partner and partnership.

The distinction between employee, partner, and independent contractor status is not insubstantial. A partner is entitled to a share of the profits of the partnership in lieu of compensation. A partner is also liable for the acts of other partners. By contrast, an employee is entitled to the compensation set forth in the agreement and is not liable for the employer's debts. An employer-employee relationship results in tax and related obligations, such as the withholding of income taxes and the payment of unemployment insurance and worker's compensation, that do not arise in the independent contractor or partnership relationship. In addition, the legal responsibility of an employer for the acts of his employee differs from the responsibility of a contracting party for the acts of independent contractors. Although the written agreement is not dispositive of the legal relationships between the parties--that is, a reviewing court could disregard the stipulation--it can be used to structure the relationship and to express the parties' intention as to its nature.

A detailed discussion of the factors used to determine whether a person is an independent contractor or an employee is beyond the scope of this chapter. Generally speaking, a court will focus on the right to control what is done and how it is done and on the nature of the work to be performed and its functional integration into the employer's ordinary business. An employer has the right to control his employee, and an employee's function is fully integrated into the employer's ordinary business. A contracting party does not have the same degree of control over an independent contractor. Because of the legal ramifications, a well-drafted personal service contract will always include a provision defining the relationship between the parties.

Whether the contract envisions an independent contractor or an employee relationship, it is a personal service contract entered into with a particular party in mind. Rights and obligations should not be assignable or transferable to other parties. This problem can be avoided most easily by including in the agreement a clause acknowledging that the services to be rendered and the obligations to be performed are special and unique and, therefore, that all the rights and obligations under the contract are personal and not assignable or transferable.

Attributes of the Parties

An important consideration when contracting with a physician or group of physicians is the attributes of the physician or physicians that attracted you to the relationship in the first place. Many times these attributes are taken for granted or assumed, but if lost or nonexistent in the first place, they could easily lessen the value of the relationship to which you bound yourself or your group. When contracting with an individual or group, it is best to define the attributes of the individual or group that will enable the parties to perform the duty under the contract in the way that you anticipate.

One of the most essential attributes of an employed physician is the ability to obtain and maintain a valid, unrestricted license in the state or states in which he will work under the employment agreement. You may want the individual also to hold specialty board certification and to obtain recertification at the time intervals dictated by the board. The individual physician with whom you are contracting should also be able to obtain unrestricted medical staff privileges in the hospitals in which you or your group practice. You may also require that there be no evidence of past disciplinary rulings from other medical staffs or licensure boards. The denial or loss of medical staff privileges might make this individual much less valuable to you, and it may be important to state in the agreement that any denial or loss of medical staff privileges at the hospitals where you or your group practice would give you the option to cancel the employment contract.

Another essential attribute is the ability of physicians to obtain malpractice insurance, possibly even at a certain premium rate.

The physician whom you are employing should agree in the contract to submit to the group's rules and regulations. We find it easier not to include in the agreement itself what could be a fair number of standing rules, but instead to reference an existing document containing such rules. The agreement, however, should contain a statement whereby the employed physician's failure to meet the requirements of the standing rules would constitute a breach of the contract or give you the option to cancel the contract.

There may be other attributes that you will require, especially if you are representing a large group employer. We have learned to examine the attributes of the existing members of the group, listing them carefully in a checklist format so that they can be addressed during negotiations and then incorporated either in the agreement or in a document referenced in the agreement.

Term

To define the term of an agreement, there must be a starting date and an ending date. It is a simple matter to state a term, but it is often ignored. Many states will statutorily limit the period for personal service contract (under which an employment contract between physicians would fall). Therefore it is important to know what is the maximum period allowed in your jurisdiction. If no period is stated, there may still be case law that supports the concept that the period must be "reasonable." The definition of "reasonable" usually requires further search into the case law. In the absence of such a definition, you might have to rely on the usual duration of such contracts in your community or your state.

The term of a contract can begin with a time and date, which is the simplest and most straightforward practice. Many times this approach is not appropriate, and you may wish to start the term with the occurrence of an event. An example would be your desire to employ a physician who is board certified but the best candidate for the position is only board eligible. A contract with this physician might state that the term of the agreement will commence 90 days after that physician submits notification of successful completion of the board examination. If you use this technique of starting or stopping a term with an event, it may be important to place some limit on the time after which the contract cannot be legally binding, even if the event or condition eventually takes place. To continue the example of the board-eligible physician, you should consider what occurs if he does not successfully pass his board examination. Would you want the contract to start 90 days after he passed his board examination on the second or even third try, possibly one or two years in the future? If you do not wish this result, it should be made clear that the agreement to employ the physician has no legal force if the individual does not pass the board examination this particular time.

Termination

The termination of contracts can also be stated by actual date and time or by an event, the latter accompanied by the same safeguards as mentioned

---

above in the discussion of starting times.

One particular event that can result in termination deserves special attention. Many medical groups find it advantageous to end a relationship when a physician attains a certain age, often 65. Many groups wish to maintain a certain vitality, which depends on adding younger members. If physicians are allowed to continue past age 65, this sometimes is thought to skew the age of the group, thereby blocking entry of younger physicians. Another reason given is that, for some of the more technically oriented specialties, it is thought that age may begin to affect performance. In order to avoid making individual decisions regarding the ability to perform, many groups arbitrarily set an age at which a physician will no longer be employed. Age as an event for termination of an employment contract can be fraught with hazard, depending on state law and whether the federal Age Discrimination in Employment Act of 1967 applies to the agreement.

In certain employment agreements there are statements concerning notification before termination and language that deals with renewal of the agreement. Notification before termination is sometimes coupled with an automatic renewal of the agreement. Such language might read as follows:

This agreement will automatically renew for a period of three years unless one party notifies the other no less than 90 days before the termination date that it wishes to terminate the agreement.

The purpose of such a statement may be to provide a method for the canceling party to remind the other party that the cancellation is to take place, thereby providing some time to make other arrangements. We usually find these types of statements to be onerous, for they can provide what we call the "notice trap." Many times, contracts are written and unfortunately forgotten. If the canceling party does not recall that there is such a notification requirement, it can find itself proscribed from canceling the contract and committed to a new term. In some jurisdictions, these renewal terms can be vitiated by the statutory limits of a personal service contract, which demand a new commitment to a binding agreement by negotiation if not by execution of another agreement. Therefore, we usually do not use notification terms or automatic renewal. Instead, we prefer to allow automatic renewal of the contract only for a term shorter than the original term and with a cancellation provision.

If notice is required as it relates either to termination or to other aspects of the contract, the method by which notice is given is important and should be defined in the agreement. Usually the place where notice is to be delivered and the times at which it can be delivered are mentioned in the agreement. In addition, the person to whom notice should be given can be indicated. The method of delivery of the notice--regular mail; certified mail, return receipt requested; or hand delivery--can be incorporated into the agreement, as well as a definition of when notice is actually received, if that is felt to be an important item. Notice can be effective on actual receipt by an individual or when postmarked. Although these factors seem to be trivial, they can help avoid misunderstanding and can be incorporated easily into agreements as "boilerplate" language, which rarely requires further negotiations between parties.

There are times when it is advantageous for employment agreements to terminate merely with notice by the canceling party. In such cases, one is well advised to specify that neither party shall incur any liability as a result of such termination. The attractiveness of a termination-at-will provision is apparent when you consider that it may not be very practical to have a disgruntled professional practicing medicine with you or your group.

Duties Performed By Each Party

Because the reason for entering into an employment agreement is to legally bind the parties to perform certain duties, the agreement should define those duties as specifically as possible. Usually we incorporate language that states that the individual physician is expected to practice medicine competently and according to accepted principles. There are other aspects of professional activity, however, that invite more detailed definitions. One such aspect is the time that the professional will give to the employer. The agreement should specify whether the physician will be a full-time or part-time employee, and the terms full-time and part-time should be defined. If you are asking a physician to work certain hours, the task of specifying the work commitment is easier. However, to apply such time strictures to most physicians would be unrealistic. We usually include general guidelines as to the usual work hours and work days. For instance, you might require a physician to be available to see patients in his clinical office from 8:00 a.m. to 5:00 p.m., five days a week, possibly even to include weekends. Further, you might want him to respond to calls at his home from patients and to meet the needs of those patients, such as seeing them in a hospital emergency department. You may also want the physician to care for patients in the hospital. Under these circumstances, it is very difficult to specify the hours and days that the physician will perform his duties. To cope with the uncertainty of the time commitment, we usually insert language into an agreement such as the following:

Since the provision of care to patients does not always occur during the usual working hours (as would be described earlier in the agreement), the physician is expected to respond to the requests and needs of patients during nonworking hours in a manner commensurate with his responsibility to those patients.

Often the parties will want to specify the nonoffice or nonworking hours more explicity and so-called on-call responsibility may have to be defined.

Another consideration in specifying the time a physician is to devote to the employer is whether the employed physician would be permitted to practice medicine at those times not committed to the employer. This is usually addressed in so-called "moonlighting clauses," either allowing or restricting extra employment activities in whole or in part. We have recently encountered a situation in which physicians, restricted to practicing medicine only for their employer, were using their medical knowledge, education, and judgment in aiding attorneys to prepare malpractice cases or product liability cases. Because these types of activities are becoming more popular with physicians, they might have to be dealt with in agreements, which could either restrict or allow such medicolegal activities.

The definition of vacation, sick, emergency, and continuing medical education leave can be expressed either in the agreement itself or by reference to another document containing such information. We find it valuable to define vacation days in terms of the number of working days so that there is no confusion as to whether Saturdays, Sundays, or holidays are to be included. A list of agreed-upon holidays is also valuable.

The scope of duties to be performed by the physician should also be addressed in the agreement. One of the major issues to be dealt with is the area of medicine in which you want the employed physician to practice. Statements limiting activity to one specialty or another may or may not be very helpful, depending on your particular situation. Certain physicians practicing a specialty may anticipate a certain scope of practice. As an example, a family practitioner may anticipate practicing obstetrics while your group may find this to be untenable in its particular medicolegal setting. If you were to hire this family physician and then inform him later that obstetrics is not to be an aspect of his practice, the agreement has failed to adequately evidence the intent of both parties. So-called specialty turf battles can also occur if agreements do not adequately spell out the intent of the parties. Assume that there are two plastic surgeons in your group and you are hiring an otolaryngologist. The otolaryngologist may be trained and competent in performing plastic procedures on the nose, and the hospital in which your group practices may be very willing to confer such operating privileges on him, but it may be the wish of your group not to have the otolaryngologist perform such procedures. Failure of the agreement to address these types of considerations can lead to some very emotionally charged confrontations within a group.

When hiring a physician, you should also anticipate whether you wish employed physicians to perform duties other than practicing medicine. You might anticipate the individual speaking to professional or lay groups as part of your marketing strategy. For example, you may wish your orthopedic surgeon to be an advisor to the boy scouts or to the school board athletics committee. Again, such activities should be anticipated and the intent of the parties made clear either in the agreement or by reference to another document that contains a discussion of these matters. If civic responsibilities are envisaged, the contract might provide that the time and energy devoted to such activities will not be permitted to interfere with the specific obligations under the contract. The matter might also be resolved by including a clause that provides that the employee shall perform additional duties as may be required by the group from time-to-time without any effect on his or her obligations under the contract.

When considering the duties you wish the party with whom you contract to perform, it is important to specify whether those duties are divisible or indivisible. If a contract containing a number of duties is divisible, it might be treated as if it were a series of contracts, each addressing one duty. If one of those duties could not be performed, it might not affect the agreement as it applied to the other duties. On the other hand, if a contract is indivisible, all the duties must be performed or the entire contract fails.

An example may add clarity to this concept. Let us say that your group employs another group that consists of a family practitioner and two general internists. The group is expected to see patients at a satellite location 10 miles from where your main group practices. The agreement was sought so that the group could provide primary care to both children and adults. After entering into the agreement, the family practitioner is unable to perform his duties, and the general internists do not feel qualified to provide pediatric care. Is the contract still valid?

If pediatric and adult care were divisible functions, the contract is still valid. If pediatric and adult care were indivisible duties, the inability of the employee group to provide pediatric care constitutes a breach of the contract. One can create many other scenarios under which one would be asking a group of individuals to provide a range of services. You must decide whether you want the contract to be valid if one or more of these services cannot be provided. This is a significant concept and one that should be thought about carefully when defining the activities that are to be performed by one or a group of employees.

By including a waiver clause, your group can retain the option to permit deviations from the agreement in some circumstances without jeopardizing its right to object in others. Such a clause generally provides that the waiver of a breach of any provision shall not operate or be construed as a waiver of any subsequent breach.

In discussions of duties, it is not long before titles become a subject. This is usually a tangential issue but one that can have significant emotional impact, because many times titles indicate duties that will be performed. A title, for instance, can refer to the type of practice in which one engages. An example might be a physician specializing in the treatment of adolescents or a physician specializing in weight control. Such a physician may wish to have his professional interests stated in a title, and this may or may not be in keeping with the practice and needs of the group. We recommend that such issues be discussed and incorporated within an agreement where advisable. There are other titles--such as department head, section head, and chairman--that designate administrative responsibilities and that also should be discussed and incorporated into an agreement when deemed appropriate.

The use of the names of the employer and the employee, before, during, or after the term of the employment, is another issue that can create potential problems. We provide in all of our contracts that the employer controls the use of its name at all times and the use of the employee's name during the term of the employment in promotional materials. At the same time, the employee is prevented from using the employer's name either during the time he is an employee or after he ends his employment. Of course, an employee may wish similar protection.

We have concentrated on the duties of the employee, because the employer's main duty is usually thought of as compensation. But there are other duties that the employer of a physician must usually perform. The provision of office space, lay personnel support, malpractice insurance, books, journals, dues, and secretarial and other business support may also need to be explicitly defined, depending on the relationship between the parties. Some groups find such explicit delineation of the employer's duties to be unnecessary or onerous and provide in the agreement a simple statement that the employer will provide all things necessary to the practice of medicine by the employee. This is usually the approach of large groups that take it for granted that they will provide all such items to an employee. Even with these groups, however, we would urge that the employer's support be discussed in the negotiation process and even evidenced in a letter or other document outside the agreement so that there is no subsequent misunderstanding. To prevent later disputes, the letter or other document should be incorporated by reference into the principal agreement.

Compensation

The usual duty of an employer is to provide compensation for the employee's efforts. It is generally appropriate to define initial compensation in the employment agreement. Changes in compensation may be addressed by reference in the agreement to the method by which they will be determined. Usually, an individual, a management committee, or a salary committee that will make the decision is identified, and an indication that the decision is final and binding is included in the agreement.

Not only should there be a statement of the initial dollar amount, but retirement benefits and any bonus provisions should be enumerated. If part of the physician's compensation is to be a share of the net profits of the group or a bonus based on net profits, the method of calculation should be included in the agreement. The timing of the disbursement should be agreed upon, as should the intervals at which changes in salary will be considered. Frequently, the agreement will provide that compensation shall be paid on the regularly scheduled pay dates of the employer and shall be subject to all appropriate withholdings or other deductions required by law or by the employer's established policies.

Furthermore, any other perquisites and fringes should be explained. We usually find these provisions to be quite cumbersome to put into an agreement and usually reference another document that lists them.

A popular method of at least partial compensation has been coming to the forefront for many of the larger groups and may become more popular in the smaller groups. Many young physicians have sizable indebtedness from their medical training and education. Other indebtedness may have been incurred if the employer lent money to the physician during his training. This usually occurs if the employer trains residents, designates a resident to take further training after completion of residency, and then hires the physician for the group in a specialized field. As part of the compensation negotiated between the employer and employee, the employer may agree to pay the loan principal owed to a third party or forgive the indebtedness for which the employer is the creditor. In the latter situation, the forgiveness of the indebtedness will usually be conditioned upon the employee's continued employment by the employer at the time when the loan payment is forgiven.

This forgiveness of indebtedness or payment of indebtedness to a third party should be explicitly agreed upon by the parties and evidenced in a written document, either as part of the employment agreement or as a separate agreement. There are significant tax ramifications when an employer pays an employee's debts or forgives debts. It is beyond the scope of this chapter to expand on these tax consequences, but both the employer and employee should be forewarned to gain expert advice when structuring such compensation schemes.

Eventual Partnership

If employment is intended to lead to eventual partnership, basic details of the partnership may, but need not, be set forth in the employment contract. A full discussion of the rights and duties of the partners, however, should be reserved for the actual partnership agreement, particularly in large, established groups.

An employment agreement between a physician or group employer and an employed physician might include the statement that the parties contemplate a partnership agreement will be executed upon termination of the employment agreement on a specific date. In a two- or three-person partnership, the parties might set out the anticipated percentage of the net income that each will receive after the partnership commences and the percentage interest in the existing professional equipment that the junior physician will purchase as a condition of partnership. The anticipated payout term could also be stated. In large partnerships in which percentages shift each time a new partner is added, such provisions would be cumbersome. If the employment contract, however, does contain terms relating to the eventual partnership, it should specify that the partnership agreement may contain such other provisions as the parties agree to at the later date. It is unlikely that all necessary elements will be included in an employment contract executed years prior to the formation of the partnership.

Restrictive Covenants

Two types of restrictive covenants have particular relevance to employee contracts with physicians. The first is the covenant not to compete, which provides that the physician-employee will refrain from engaging in the practice of medicine, or in a particular subspecialty, in a certain geographical region for a specified period following the termination of his employment.

Noncompetition clauses are viewed with suspicion by the courts because, by definition, they are in restraint of trade. In some jurisdictions, any agreement that purports to limit a physician's ability to practice his profession is considered against public policy and nonenforceable. Even in jurisdictions without a blanket prohibition on agreements restricting a physician's right to practice, not all agreements with that aim will be enforced. State laws usually permit only those noncompetition clauses that are reasonable in scope and that are not unduly harmful to the parties or the public.

A noncompetition clause might also be subject to federal antitrust laws, most particularly the Sherman Act. The Sherman Act proscribes, among other things, contracts that restrain trade or commerce. Medical practice has been held to be a trade for purposes of the Sherman Act. Federal antitrust law applies when the contract at issue affects interstate commerce. To determine whether interstate commerce is affected by a physician's employment agreement, a court will consider whether revenue flows to the physician from federally funded sources or out-of-state payers, whether supplies and equipment are ordered by the physician from out-of-state, and whether patients travel across state lines to receive treatment from the physician. As with state law, Sherman Act analysis focuses on the reasonableness of the challenged provision.

The "reasonableness" and, therefore, validity of a restrictive covenant in a physician employment contract will be determined by considering the effects of the restriction on the parties and the public, the presence and extent of territorial and time limitations, and the scope of the covered activities. As a general matter, a reasonable covenant imposes only the degree of restraint that is necessary to protect the interest of the physician-employer.

Assume that a group of psychiatrists employs a new associate on the condition that, for a period of five years after termination of his employment, he will not deliver services to any client he served as an employee. One of the group's corporate clients employs the associate on a full-time basis after his termination, but continues to utilize the consultative services of the group. In an analogous situation, a federal court ruled that the noncompetition clause was not enforceable because it was broader than was necessary to protect the employer's legitimate interests. See *Wilson v. Clarke*, 470 F.2d 1218 (1st Cir. 1972).

A covenant that totally prohibits an employed physician from using his skill and knowledge as a physician also would be invalid, as it imposes too great a hardship on the employed physician. Let us suppose a gastroenterologist employs an associate, pursuant to an agreement that the associate refrain from practicing both general internal medicine and gastroenterology in the area covered by the employer's practice for three years after termination. The agreement would be overbroad in its proscription against the practice of internal medicine. See *Karpinski v. Ingrasci*, 28 N.Y. 2d 45, 268 N.E. 2d 751 (1971). Noncompetition convenants should be limited to the type of practice engaged in by the employer.

In a small community where a restrictive covenant might leave an insufficient number of physicians, a court generally will not enforce an agreement not to practice medicine within the region. A noncompetition clause prohibiting the only orthopedic surgeon in the region from practicing orthopedic surgery might be unenforceable because it would impose too great a hardship on the public.

Frequently, a reviewing court will consider time and territory jointly. A covenant limited to the area of the physician-employer's practice would be reasonable, even if the restriction applied for an extended period. A shorter period may permit a restraint that covers a greater territory. There is some support for the view that, if an area is too broad or a period too long, a court will rewrite the agreement and enforce it over a reasonable territory and for a reasonable period.

A physician-employee may also be prohibited from using his former employer's list of patients and from soliciting such patients, provided that this restriction is clearly set forth in the contract. Because restrictive covenants are not favored by the courts, they will be strictly construed against the employer. The language, therefore, should be comprehensive and concise.

The usual remedy for a breach of a restrictive covenant is an action for damages or for an injunction. The measure of damages is the actual amount of the loss and injuries sustained by the physician-employer as a direct and immediate result of the breach. Punitive damages are generally not available. To eliminate the uncertainty associated with remedial relief, the parties should consider stipulating in the agreement the sum to be paid as damages. The stipulation will be upheld as long as it is determined to be based on liquidated damages and not as a penalty or punishment for the breach.

The law governing the reasonableness and validity of restrictive convenants varies widely from jurisdiction to jurisdiction. A local attorney should be consulted if you wish to include this type of covenant in a physician employment contract.

The second type of restriction that might be included in a physician employment contract is a clause regarding the physician-employee's inventions and patents. In the absence of an agreement to the contrary, a physician under a general employment agreement is vested with the ownership of his or her inventions. The group or physician-employer does not have any right to the inventions of the physician-employee even though, in order to perfect the invention, the physician-employee used the employer's property, received assistance from others in the group, or utilized time on the invention that otherwise would have been devoted to the group's practice, and would not have had the knowledge or means to make the invention were it not for the employer.

The group can change this result by providing in the contract that it will be entitled to inventions or discoveries made during the term of employment. The employment contract might provide that the physician-employee is entitled to additional compensation for inventions or for the use of inventions or royalties from any patent entered into by the group. The group may also wish to ask the employee to agree in his employment contract to assign inventions conceived by him both during the course of employment and for a reasonable time thereafter, providing the invention stems from work done while with the group. Agreements of this nature may also be executed outside the employment contract, provided that the physician-employee receives some benefit from the employer in connection with the execution of the agreement. As is the case with a covenant not to compete, an agreement not to assign inventions for an indefinite period following the termination of employment may be invalid if it is overbroad.

To protect the group or employer-physician from possible invalidity of one or both of the restrictive covenants or of any other general provision in the contract, the agreement should recite that, if any portion of the agreement is found to be void or illegal, the validity or enforceability of any other portion shall not be affected. A clause that permits the severance of invalid or unenforceable terms minimizes the possibility that the entire contract will be rendered unenforceable by the inclusion of one or more terms later found to be invalid.

Breach of the Contract

A contract is breached when either party fails to perform a contractual duty, unless nonperformance is legally justified. Assume that Dr. Bailey and Acme Medical Group enter into an employment agreement in which Dr. Bailey agrees to see patients at the Acme Medical Group's clinic from Monday through Friday between the hours of 9:00 a.m. and 5:30 p.m. Dr. Bailey then instructs the scheduling clerk that he will not see patients on Wednesdays, because he plans to play golf on that day. Dr. Bailey has breached the contract. If, however, Dr. Bailey refused to see patients on Wednesdays because the clinic building was closed and normal, necessary services were not provided to his office, his nonperformance would be justified, and there would be no breach.

An unexcused failure to perform constitutes a breach only when the duty to perform has arisen. An absolute duty is one that is unconditional and independent of any other event. Let us assume that Dr. Bailey is a much sought after young surgeon. To induce him to agree to work with the Acme Medical Group, it promises him a $25,000 bonus on the date he signs an employment contract. When Dr. Bailey signs the agreement, the group's duty to pay becomes absolute. Its failure to pay, absent some legal justification, would constitute a breach. But, suppose that the group's promise to pay the signing bonus was conditioned upon Dr. Bailey's physical relocation to Cincinnati where the Group's offices are located. Dr. Bailey signs the contract, but fails to make the move. The Group's failure to pay the signing bonus in this circumstance is not a breach. Its promise was conditional, and the condition was not fulfilled.

A condition is defined as an act or event, other than a mere lapse of time, that affects a duty to perform. The duty to perform the promised act is dependent on an independent event. Unless the condition is fulfilled, the duty is not absolute. Conditions can be classified according to the time when the conditioning event is to occur in relation to the duty to perform. A condition precedent must occur before a duty to perform arises. In our second example, Dr. Bailey's relocation was a precedent condition. A concurrent condition is one that must occur simultaneously with the duty to perform the promised act. Concurrent conditions exist principally in sales contracts. A subsequent condition is one that operates to discharge a duty of performance after it becomes absolute. True subsequent conditions are rare. We can envisage a situation, however, in which a physician-employee's agreement not to compete with his physician-employer would be conditioned on the physician-employer's continued practice in the geographic area.

Conditions can be further classified as express or constructive. Express conditions are those that are clearly spelled out in the contract or that can be implied from the terms of the contract. In physician employment contract, the duty to employ is either explicitly or implicitly subject to the physician's obtaining a license to practice in the relevant state. Explicit conditions must be complied with literally, or a duty to perform does not arise.

Constructive conditions are neither expressed in nor implied from the terms of the contract. They are imposed by law to prevent unjust enrichment or otherwise to do justice. Such conditions must be complied with substantially, rather than literally. In the context of employment contracts, courts are likely to impose constructive conditions when personal services have been rendered and payment has not been made.

Contract provisions commencing with words such as "if", "on condition that," "subject to," or "provided" create conditions to performance. These conditions are express and must be literally complied with before a duty to perform arises. And, an absolute, unconditional duty to perform must arise before a breach can occur. Once a duty becomes absolute, a failure to perform or a performance that does not comply with the terms of the contract will constitute a breach, absent some justification rendering performance impossible.

One might choose to include a provision granting the breaching party a period to correct the error or breach before the complaining party can take legal action. Such clauses, however, are rare in employment contracts, which generally are terminable at the will of either party.

In the U.S. system, a legal remedy exists for every legal wrong. Accordingly, an injured party has a cause of action for every breach of contract. The injured party is entitled to be compensated for the actual damages suffered, or if none are proved, for nominal damages. He might also be entitled to an injunction prohibiting a continuing breach if he can show irreparable harm. In addition, the breaching party loses the benefit of the bargain; the injured party is relieved of any further obligation to perform. Specific performance, a remedy in which the court orders the breaching party to perform the contract, is not available for the breach of an employment or other personal service contract.

Actions for damages in connection with employment contracts arise most frequently in two contexts: an employee sues an employer for wrongful discharge, assuming employment was terminable only for cause or only after a certain period, and an employer seeking damages for wrongful termination of employment by the employee, when a contract is for a specified time. In the former context, the measure of damages is the salary to which the employee would have been entitled during the remainder of the term reduced by the income that he has earned, or will earn, during the unexpired term. Some states also recognize tort actions for wrongful discharge, even in an employment-at-will situation.

When an employee wrongfully terminates employment, the employer is generally entitled to recover any additional cost of obtaining substitute help for the contract term. Although most jurisdictions recognize a duty to mitigate damages, by seeking comparable employment, for example, we advise that the employment contract include a clause requiring the physician-employee to mitigate any damages to which he or she may be entitled under the contract.

The above summary assumes that the employment agreement does not address damages or the means for determining damages. When an employment contract contains a covenant not to compete, one would be well advised to include a clause in which the physician-employee acknowledges that breach of the covenant is likely to result in irreparable harm to the employer and consents to temporary and permanent injunctive relief, in addition to other available remedies, to prevent the commission or continuation of a breach of the obligation not to compete. An employer may also wish to provide in the contract that he is entitled to recover any profits the physician-employee may have obtained in violation of the agreement, as well as attorneys' fees and litigation expenses. If specific remedies are stated, the clause should always provide that the specified remedies are in addition to all other remedies available in law or in equity.

A medical group or physician-employer may wish to avoid the necessity of going to court to obtain a remedy for breach of contract. In this instance, the contract can provide for arbitration of any controversies or claims. Judgment on the arbitrator's award may be rendered in any court having jurisdiction over the parties and the matter. An arbitration clause is not self-executing. To avoid disputes over the method by which the arbitration is to proceed, the contract should specify the ground rules or incorporate by reference the rules of the American Association of Arbitration. Even in contracts providing for arbitration of disputes, however, the employer should reserve the right to seek temporary or permanent injunctive relief for a breach or threatened breach of a covenant not to compete.

External Constraints

One of the guiding principles of the U.S. legal system is freedom of contract. The goal of the courts in contract disputes is to ascertain the intent of the parties, which are often obscured by unclear or imprecise language in written agreements or conflicting, faulty memory in oral agreements. Nonetheless, both state and federal law impose some restraints on an individual's freedom to contract. A court will not enforce a contract with an illegal purpose. For example, if a medical group entered into a contract with an unlicensed practitioner for the practice of medicine, the unlicensed practitioner could not enforce the agreement because the unauthorized practice of medicine violates state law. And a contract that results in a violation of federal or state antitrust laws is not enforceable.

Similarly, an employment agreement will not shield an employer who discriminates against persons on the basis of their race, sex, religion, or national origin in violation of Title VII of the Civil Rights Act of 1964. Federal law in the guise of the Age Discrimination in Employment Act of 1967 (ADEA), and corresponding state law in many jurisdictions, also prohibits discrimination against individuals between forty (40) and seventy (70) years of age. ADEA applies to all employers that employ 20 or more employees. Its application to partnerships with more than 20 partners but fewer than 20 employees has not been resolved.

Reduced to its simplest terms, ADEA proscribes employment decisions in hiring, firing, benefits, or other terms and conditions of employment based on age between 40 and 70, unless age is a bona fide occupational qualification reasonably necessary to the normal operation of the employer's business or unless the decision is made pursuant to a bona fide seniority system or employee benefit plan. Further, the law prohibits employee benefit plans that require or permit involuntary retirement before the age of 70, except in certain specified instances in which the employee is between 65 and 70 years of age and for two years prior to retirement has served in an executive or high policy-making position. Nothing in the law prohibits discharge of an employee in the protected age group for good cause.

In the example set out in the section of this chapter addressing termination, the forced retirement of a 65-year-old physician employee would be unlawful, unless ADEA did not apply. The group's decision can be justified if it can show that age less than 65 is a bona fide occupational qualification for the practice of medicine. Similar decisions are lawful even if ADEA applies if they are based on reasonable factors other than age, including but not limited to business cutbacks, elimination of a position, or poor performance.

The law is unsettled regarding what must be proved to establish that age is a bond fide occupational qualification. The majority view as of this writing is that the employer must show either that substantially all persons over the particular age are unable to perform the required tasks safely and efficiently, or that some older persons have traits precluding safe and efficient performance unascertainable other than through knowledge of the person's age. A definitive application of this test to physicians has not yet occurred. If the ADEA applies to your group and you are contemplating a forced retirement policy for physicians below the age of 70, you should consult your attorney.

Chapter 3

CONTRACTS BETWEEN PHYSICIANS AND HOSPITALS

Dale H. Cowan, MD, JD

Dale H. Cowan, MD, JD, is a practicing physician and attorney. He has a private medical practcie in hematology and medical oncology and is Director of the Division of Hematology/Oncology at Marymount Hospital, Cleveland, Ohio. He serves as legal counsel to medical staffs and has counseled both hospitals and physician groups in such areas as contracting with alternative health care delivery systems, privileging and credentialing, and medical staff bylaws.

Dr. Cowan played a major role in establishing a physician-sponsored preferred provider organization at Marymount Hospital and helped create the Emerald Park Network, one of the major PPO networks in the Greater Cleveland Area.

Dr. Cowen has spoken at many conferences sponsored by medical, legal, and governmental organizations on physician contracting, privileging and credentialing, and the role of physicians and medcial staffs in the changing health care environment. He has written numerous articles on these issues in the medical and legal literature; authored a book, Preferred Provider Organizations, *published by Aspen Publishers, Inc.; and coedited a book,* Human Organ Transplantation, *published by Health Administration Press. Dr. Cowan is Editor of a monthly newsletter,* Medical Staff Management, *published by Rynd Communications, National Health Publishing, and serves on the editorial board of the Hastings Center publication* IRB.

Dr. Cowan is a Clinical Professor of Environmental Health Sciences and an Associate of the Health Systems Management Center at Case Western Reserve University. He received his undergraduate and medical degrees from Harvard University and his juris doctor degree from Case Western Reserve University School of Law.

The purpose of agreements between physicians and hospitals is to formalize new or preexisting relationships between the parties. The unique needs and goals of the parties should shape the course of the negotiations and the terms of the contract. Contracts should not dictate or lead to goals or results that neither party wants.

Needs and goals that should govern the drafting of physician contracts with

---

hospitals include provision of adequate patient care, management of costs under varying reimbursement schemes, responsibility for administration and teaching, medical staff affinity, and amicable physician-hospital relationships.

Selection of the proper physician or group of physicians is probably the most important step in creating a successful contractual relationship.

Purpose of a Written Contract

Formal written contracts serve several purposes. They establish the legal relationship between the parties and state the terms and conditions of the rights and obligations of the parties. They confirm the understanding and intentions of the parties when they enter the relationship and, presumably, as they operate under the contract. They eliminate uncertainties regarding mutual rights, obligations, and relationships, and protect against future disputes.

Additionally, written contracts have significant legal implications with respect to decisions and actions of external agencies, such as regulatory agencies, accreditation bodies, taxation authorities, federal and state reimbursement agencies, third-party payers, and competitors.

Finally, the process of agreeing on specific terms and conditions provides an opportunity for the parties to establish a working relationship based on openness, good faith, and reasonableness.

It is often desirable for the hospital to use a standard general form of contract for all physicians. Standard contracts are easier for the hospital to administer, eliminate time-consuming and often arduous negotiations, and enable the hospital to achieve consistency in the administration of its policies. Additionally, standard contracts minimize the risk that particularly favorable terms accorded one physician or physician group will engender resentment on the part of other physicians and impair the hospital's credibility in future negotiations.

However, it is important that parties seeking to use standard contracts avoid appearing rigid and inflexible. Rather, they should be prepared to modify standard terms and conditions to accommodate special or unusual circumstances that might arise.

Negotiations

The process of negotiating the contract is of considerable value to the parties and sets the tone for the relationship. Negotiations that are bitter, antagonistic, or adversarial may well doom a relationship from the outset.

In starting the negotiations, the opening position of each party is paramount.

It sets the tone and the parameters for all future negotiations. Attitudes that reflect good faith and reasonableness can facilitate the negotiating process and establish a positive basis for future good relations. It is useful to enter the negotiations with the attitude and expectation that a mutually satisfying long-term agreement and relationship will result.

Because contracts are legal documents, it is important that they be written in appropriate legal language. For this reason, they should be prepared by competent legal counsel. However, attorneys need not negotiate on behalf of the parties. Indeed, having attorneys negotiate for the parties may slow the process and generate distrust among persons who should be getting to know each other. However, legal counsel should review the agreed upon terms to ensure they reflect the intent and goals of the parties and to identify intended and unintended implications.

If someone other than the party to the contract is negotiating for the other side, it is important to determine that person's authority before starting the negotiations. It is preferable that the person negotiating for the other party have the same authority for agreeing to terms one's own negotiator has. It can be frustrating and time-consuming to negotiate with someone who lacks the authority to enter into an agreement.

Effective negotiating requires ample advance preparation. Before adopting a position in a negotiation, a party should have data and reasons substantiating and justifying the position. Such preparation should also identify issues or points the party is not prepared to discuss. It is important that these latter issues not be negotiated.

Ordinarily, it is preferable to start negotiations with easy issues and to stress points of agreement between the parties. This fosters good will and provides momentum for subsequent negotiations. Essential terms should not be left ambiguous merely to reach agreement. Rather, it is important to arrive at an acceptable compromise on all issues that are potentially explosive and that could surface later. Although the party that prepares the initial draft of an agreement has the advantage of filling in any gaps or ambiguities in its favor, ambiguous terms are often construed *against* that party.

It is advisable never to present a position as a "final" offer unless you are prepared to terminate negotiations in the event that the position is not accepted. A party that modifies a "final" offer risks losing credibility.

Finally, it is useful to understand the other party's needs and goals. Although such understanding should not lead one to abandon one's own needs and goals, it should facilitate agreement on terms that are acceptable to both sides. A one-sided agreement is not indicative of successful negotiations, because it may lead to future disputes and to a breakdown in the relationship between the parties. The best contract is one that is fair and satisfies both parties' key interests.

Relationship Between the Parties

Physicians who contract with hospitals to provide professional services can enter into either of two relationships with the institution: independent contractor or employee. It is not always easy to determine if one is an employee or an independent contractor. The status of the hospital physician contractee will be determined by the actual circumstances surrounding the relationship and not necessarily by how the parties characterize the relationship. Nonetheless, it is important to identify employees and independent contractors, because tax, reimbursement, and other statutes and regulations affect employers, employees, and independent contractors differently.

Definitions

The determining consideration in distinguishing an employee from an independent contractor is control. An *independent contractor* is a person who contracts to perform work for another party according to the individual's own methods and without being subject to that party's supervision except as to the results or the end product of the work. An *employee* is a person in the service of another under any contract of hire, written or oral, whereby the employer has the power or right to control and direct the employee in the material details of how the work is to be performed.

The basic difference between the independent contractor and the employee is that the latter is not permitted to exercise discretion in providing the service either as to the means utilized or to the work product itself. In general, a physician is properly regarded as a hospital employee rather than as an independent contractor if the hospital retains the right to control the time, manner, and method of accomplishing the desired result rather then merely the right to require definite results in conformity to a contract. Where the right to control exists, the actual exercise of such control is not important.

In addition to exercising control over the judgment and performance of the employee, other indicia of the employment relationship include payment of wages, payment for the period of work rather than for the services performed, termination at will (now circumscribed by the courts in many jurisdictions), the nature and status of the occupation, the providing of tools and supplies, withholding and payment of income and Social Security taxes and unemployment coverage, and the intent and understanding of the parties. Additional factors suggesting a physician is an employee rather than an independent contractor include restrictions on all outside practice of the physician and compensation by the hospital of all substitute physicians who work while the contracting physician is absent.

In its determinations whether a physician is an employee or independent contractor, the Internal Revenue Service (IRS) has focused on the question of whether the hospital controls, or has a right to control, the physician and whether the hospital can hire or fire the physician at will. The IRS said, in Revenue Ruling 72-203:

"Physicians who engage in the pursuit of an independent medical practice in which they offer their services to the public are generally independent contractors and not employees. However, if the requisite control and supervision over a physician exist with respect to services performed for another, he is an employee rather than an independent contractor. Whether the requisite control and supervision exist is determined by the application of such factors as:

■ The degree to which the individual has become integrated into the operating organization of the person or firm for which the services are performed.

■ The substantial nature, regularity, and continuity of his work for such person or firm.

■ The authority vested in or reserved by such person or firm to require compliance with its general policies.

■ The degree to which the individual under consideration has been accorded the rights and privileges that the firm has created or established for its employees generally."

Certain provisions of the recently enacted Tax Reform Act of 1986 (P.L. 99-514) may affect the status of a contracting physician as an independent contractor. The reader is advised to consult a tax expert with respect to such applicable provisions.

Statements in the contract can help determine whether a physician is an employee or independent contractor. However, they are not necessarily conclusive. The determining factor for courts and administrative agencies is how the parties actually treat each other. Nonetheless, it is important for the parties to spell out the nature of the relationship as clearly as possible, because courts and agencies give serious consideration to the language of the contract when faced with a physician of uncertain status.

Considerations that Affect Whether to Adopt an Employment or Independent Contractor Arrangement

There are numerous factors that affect the determination of whether a relationship between a hospital and a physician or group of physicians should be in the form of an employment or an independent contractor arrangement. These factors include business, professional, regulatory, reimbursement, and tax considerations.

Control

A major consideration affecting the choice of arrangement between the hospital and the physician is the matter of control. Adoption of an independent contractor arrangement will reduce the ability of the hospital to control and exercise responsibility for the practice of medicine in its facilities. Independent contractors must be accorded sufficient autonomy to protect their legal status. Too much control by the hospital may jeopardize the independent contractor status. Too little control, however, may weaken the ability of the governing board and medical staff to enforce their standards and policies and may endanger the facility's tax-exempt status. Too little control may also interfere with the hospital's responsibility for monitoring and managing quality control and for providing for institutional management and planning.

In order to protect itself, the hospital may seek to exercise some influence over the hiring, retention, and dismissal of all associates by the contracting physician without interfering with the latter's exercising autonomous professional judgment. Alternatively, the hospital may seek an employment agreement, because such an arrangement enhances the hospital's ability to control the details of the physician's treatment of patients.

Outside Practice

The ability to practice medicine outside the hospital is another consideration determining the nature of the relationship between the hospital and the physician. An employment arrangement enhances the ability of the hospital to control or prevent the physician from practicing outside the hospital or from competing with the hospital once employment is terminated. By contrast, an independent contractor arrangement lessens the hospital's ability to control or prevent the physician from practicing outside the hospital.

Although the hospital may seek to prohibit the physician's practice of medicine elsewhere if it competes with the hospital's services or reduces the time the physician would otherwise spend providing services at the hospital, stringent restrictions on outside practice may allow the IRS or courts to take the position that the physician is an employee rather than an independent contractor.

Liability for Malpractice and Negligence

Although rules vary from state to state, hospitals are usually not liable for malpractice and negligence of independent contractors. The reason for this is that hospitals lack power of control over the professional conduct of physicians who are independent contractors. An exception to this general rule may be found in specific circumstances such as emergency room physicians. In one case, the court found a hospital liable for the actions of physicians who were independent contractors. Because the hospital held itself out to the public as offering emergency care, the patient had no choice in selecting the physician, and the public reasonably perceived that services were rendered by hospital employees and not independent contractors.

Adamski v. Tacoma General Hospital, 579 P. 2d 970 (Wash. 1978). Another exception may be where the independent contractor physician is performing various administrative tasks for the hospital, such as purchasing supplies or arranging for the treatment of patients off the hospital's premises.

By contrast, a hospital will be responsible for the malpractice and negligent acts of physicians who are employees of the hospital. Because of this, a decision to establish an employment relationship with a physician should not be made before assessing the risk and the insurance cost involved in hiring the physician.

Regardless of whether an arrangement with a physician is based on employment or independent contractor status, a hospital is independently liable for its own negligent act in entering into an agreement with a physician it knew or should have known was not competent to fulfill the clinical privileges granted or undertake the duties required, or in failing to undertake appropriate peer review of the physician's performance.

Medical Staff Relationships

Hospital contracts with physicians can affect or be affected by relationships with other members of the medical staff. A physician hired by the hospital may be identified as a "hospital" physician and not be accepted by the medical staff. Or, contractual relationships may create jurisdictional disputes with other members of the medical staff.

Potential conflicts can be avoided or overcome by careful planning and by involving the medical staff in the process of identifying the need for a particular physician or a particular service. It is important also to determine that the arrangement is consistent with the medical staff's bylaws, rules, and regulations, and that the agreement is carefully drafted to include jurisdictional definitions. Finally, the agreement should provide for a mechanism to resolve disputes that is consistent with the medical staff's bylaws.

The Market and the Type, Size, and Resources of the Hospital

The decision to employ a physician or enter into an independent contractor arrangement can be affected by the market and by the type, size, and resources of the hospital. The availability of qualified physicians who are willing to work for a hospital as salaried employees will affect an institution's bargaining options. For example, large teaching hospitals or those with large endowments may prefer, and be in a better position to insist on, an employment relationship. Small hospitals, particularly those in rural areas, or hospitals with limited resources may only be able to obtain needed services through agreements with independent contractors.

Municipal, state, and federal hospitals may require that specific services be provided only by employed physicians. However, in some jurisdictions, state laws prohibiting the corporate practice of medicine may disallow the direct employment of physicians, with the result that only independent contractor arrangements are permissible. Thus, considerations outside the control of hospitals may dictate the nature of the arrangement that can be established.

Conflicting Policies

Conflicts may exist between the policies and obligations of hospitals and those of the physician or physician group with which the hospital wishes to contract. Institutions with religious affiliations may wish or be required to restrict agreements to physicians who are members of that religion. Catholic hospitals may find that their ethical and religious obligations conflict with the obligations of a physician or group of physicians that provides services to an outside agency that provides abortion counseling. Such conflicts may prevent the formation of any arrangement between the parties.

Corporate Practice of Medicine

Some states prohibit corporations, including not-for-profit hospitals, from employing physicians and retaining profits from the physicians' services. In those states, physicians who assist a corporation to practice medicine risk having their professional licenses revoked. Employed physicians in those jurisdictions can be accused of unprofessional conduct and fee-splitting. Advice of counsel is generally required to determine whether employment relationships can be structured that do not violate the state laws. The provisions of state laws prohibiting the corporate practice of medicine may restrict hospital contracts with physicians to independent contractor arrangements. Specific state laws must therefore be carefully examined on this point.

Labor and Employment Laws

A variety of state and federal labor and employment laws apply to the employment relationship but do not protect independent contractors. For example, federal and state laws require employers to withhold federal and state income taxes and make payments for Social Security, unemployment compensation, and workers' compensation. No such obligation applies to independent contractors.

Salaried physicians are generally entitled to participate in the hospital's pension plan and to receive the same fringe benefits that are offered to other employees, including hospitalization, sick pay, vacation pay, disability insurance, and malpractice insurance. Hospitals need not offer these benefits to independent contractors. An estimate of the costs of these benefits should be made to enable the parties to calculate the relative costs of the alternative types of arrangements.

Additionally, antidiscrimination statutes and their accompanying regulations apply to a hospital's relations with employed physicians but not to independent contractors. Thus, a disgruntled physician employee can file a complaint with a federal or state agency alleging that an unfavorable action was predicated on race, age, sexual preference, marital status, etc., rather than on performance or competency. The cost of defending an action can be high in terms of money, time, morale, and adverse publicity. Similar complaints ordinarily cannot be brought by independent contractors under state or federal laws.

Regulatory Agency Relationships

State regulation of hospitals' rates, budgets, new services, and capital expenditures can affect the decision to pursue an employment arrangement or to contract with an independent contractor. For example, a state cost commission may have jurisdiction over the fees charged by hospitals for the services provided by employed physicians, such as pathologists, radiologists, and anesthesiologists. However, the commission may have no jurisdiction over the fees charged for these services when they are provided and billed separately by independent contractors who assume the attendant risks for their actions.

In another area, certification-of-need (CON) laws of some states apply only to capital expenditures by health care institutions and not to those expended by private practitioners. Institutions interested in developing or expanding services, such as magnetic resonance imaging (MRI), may be restrained from doing so by their state CON laws. No such impediment may restrict development or expansion carried out by physicians who are independent contractors. Hospitals may thereby be able to implement strategic plans through their arrangements with independent contractors that might otherwise not be approved.

Similarly, federal laws that control hospitals' charges and costs may restrict development that can be undertaken by independent physicians or groups of physicians.

Tax Considerations

Tax considerations for employment contracts are considerably simpler than for independent contractor arrangements. Perhaps the most important issue is the exemption from federal, state, and local laws for hospitals organized as charitable, not-for-profit corporations. Charitable exemption under federal tax laws depends on the absence of private benefit. To qualify for charitable exemption, not-for-profit hospitals must be organized and operated exclusively for charitable purposes and not for the benefit of private interests. Additionally, no part of the net earnings of charitable hospitals can inure to the benefit of private individuals.

A hospital's tax exemption is not jeopardized by payments of compensation to employed physicians. In contrast, payments to non-employed physicians may be scrutinized closely by the IRS. Factors that may be considered include the extent of support from public donations, the presence or absence of public control on the governing board, whether the independent contractor physicians are on the governing board, and the method and amount of compensation. Whereas physicians must retain control over their activities in order to be classified as independent contractors, relinquishment of control by the hospital may jeopardize its tax exemption.

Other tax issues arise with respect to payment of federal, state, and local income taxes; Social Security payments; unemployment and disability benefits; worker's compensation obligations, real and personal property taxes; sale, lease, and service taxes; and the issuance of tax-exempt bonds for financing facilities. These issues can be complex and require the advice of counsel so that terms can be drafted that promote and safeguard the interests of both parties to the agreement.

Reimbursement

One of the most important and complex issues that affect the choice of arrangement to be created between a hospital and a physician or group of physicians is that of reimbursement (or, more accurately, payment). Hospitals receive the major portion of their revenues from third-party payers, including government programs, private insurers, and other private payers.

In particular, Medicare and Medicaid regulations significantly affect hospitals' reimbursement for physicians' services. Nearly all hospitals receive payment for most inpatient services (Medicare part A) under the Prospective Payment System (PPS). The PPS provides a fixed payment per discharge based on the diagnosis-related groups (DRGs) used by Medicare. In contrast, Part B payments are made according to the prevailing and customary charges that are rendered for professional services in the community. As a consequence, there is an incentive for hospitals to reduce inpatient costs as much as possible and to maximize Part B revenues.

Medicare regulations are specific in defining the services provided by hospital-based physicians, such as radiologists, pathologists, and anesthesiologists, that are covered by Part A and Part B. The regulations also do not allow physicians to bill for Part A services and place Reasonable Compensation Equivalent (RCE) restrictions on the amount of physician services to hospitals that are reimbursable. These and related regulations affect the extent of reimbursement hospitals receive for physicians' services under employment agreements and independent contractor arrangements. It is advisable, therefore, for both physicians and hospitals to consult with specialists familiar with Medicare regulations to assess the impact of the regulations on alternative contracting arrangements and to ensure that the specific terms of an agreement are consistent with applicable policies and regulations.

In the usual situation, reimbursement considerations will not be a controlling factor in deciding whether to enter into an employment or independent contractor arrangement. Rather, the requirements of the regulations will influence the terms and conditions of the agreement.

Independent Contractor Agreement

The preceding discussion emphasized the major issues and considerations in determining whether to establish an employment or an independent contractor arrangement. Once agreement is reached as to the type of arrangement into which the parties wish to enter, a written contract should be drafted. It is important that the terms and provisions of the contract be carefully drafted so that the parties can achieve their goals and avoid penalties or other adverse consequences.

The provisions that should be included in independent contractor arrangements are presented here together with representative language.

Heading and Parties

The initial section of the agreement states exactly who the contracting parties are, their proper names, and their locations. It also indicates the legal status of the parties.

This agreement is made and entered into the _____ day of _____, 198_, by and between _____ Hospital, a nonprofit hospital corporation organized under the laws of the State of _____ and located in _____ (the "Hospital"), and _____ Corporation, Inc., a professional corporation located in _____ (the "Corporation").

Recitals

The recitals, generally starting with the word, "Whereas," explain what service is being provided under the agreement and why the parties wish to contract with each other. If the contract is an exclusive services arrangement, it is important to indicate the business reasons for the agreement in order to minimize or protect against challenges to the arrangement under federal or state antitrust laws. Although generally self-serving, the recitals can aid courts in interpreting the agreement.

WHEREAS, as a full-service acute care Hospital, the Hospital provides emergency care services for the community through the Emergency Department; and

WHEREAS, the Hospital has determined that the Emergency Department can be most efficiently administered and operated most effectively by one medical professional corporation and that effective delivery of emergency care services requires the management and marketing of such services with particular attention to the interest of the community served by the Hospital, the provision and improvement of the quality of patient care by the proper staffing of physicians, the establishment and monitoring of professional performance to assure quality care for all patients, the provision of continuous professional services, the controlling of costs, the provision of professional services to all patients in a timely manner, the provision of effective and efficient medical audit and

---

professional review procedures; and

WHEREAS, the Hospital has determined the foregoing goals may be met most effectively and the Emergency Department may be administered most efficiently by a professional medical corporation headed by a physician with experience and training in the field of emergency medicine; and

WHEREAS, the Corporation has retained the services of _____, M.D. as its President and Chief Operating Officer, herein after referred to as "Physician", duly licensed by the State of _____ Board of Medical Examiners and registered as a physician and board certified in Emergency Medicine pursuant to the laws of the State of _____; and

WHEREAS, the Parties realize that certain services and facilities (as hereinafter stated) will be provided to the Corporation by the Hospital in order to (1) realize economies resulting from the use of better purchasing arrangements and general administrative expertise of the Hospital, and (2) relieve the Corporation of the nonmedical demands placed upon professional time in connection with such services and facilities;

NOW, THEREFORE in consideration of the mutual covenants and promises contained herein, the Parties hereby agree as follows:

Definitions

Definitions can be useful in providing specific meanings to important terms used throughout the agreement in order to avoid possible ambiguity. They can also define what is meant by or included within specific services such as diagnostic imaging, therapeutic radiology, nuclear medicine, anatomic pathology, and clinical pathology.

Appointment

The agreement should contain a short, simple statement that indicates the position to which the physician or professional corporation is appointed. This section should also include a general statement of the duties the physician or corporation is expected to undertake.

This statement should be consistent with the bylaws of the medical staff. Additionally, if appropriate, it should include a statement of the physician's eligibility for membership on the medical staff and for clinical privileges and of the approval required from the hospital's governing board.

If the hospital wishes to contract for the services of a particular physician in a group, this section should indicate that that individual's services are an essential condition of the agreement.

This contract shall be in effect and binding upon the Parties upon appointment of Physician as Director of the _____ Department as approved by the

Hospital's Board of Trustees pursuant to all requirements of the Hospital's Medical Staff Bylaws and execution of this contract by both Parties hereto.

Physician agrees to provide administrative and professional ___ services required for the operation of the Department. In connection therewith, Physician, as Director of the ___ Department shall assume and discharge full and complete responsibility for the direction and management of the Department and for the provision of ___ Services in accordance with the provisions of this Agreement.

However, the medical corporation may wish to avoid any provision that gives the hospital authority to condition the agreement on the employment by the corporation of a particular physician and the availability of that physician to provide the services called for under the contract.

Medical Staff Privileges

It is essential for the agreement to specify that all contracting physicians must be admitted to the medical staff and granted clinical privileges according to the credentialing standards and procedures set out in the medical staff bylaws. It should be further stated that continuation of the agreement is contingent upon the physician remaining a member in good standing of the medical staff. Appointment to the medical staff should not come about by virtue of the contract itself.

A similar requirement should apply to physicians who are providing contracted services as employees of the professional corporation that is party to the agreement. The agreement should specify that all such physicians must qualify for medical staff membership and clinical privileges according to the medical staff's credentialing standards and procedures.

A controversy exists whether medical staff membership and clinical privileges of physicians who are independent contractors, particularly those having an exclusive arrangement with the hospital, should be coextensive with the term of the agreement and terminate when the agreement terminates. Hospital counsel generally argue that in order to accomplish the hospital's goals of economy, administrative efficiency, and quality control, medical staff membership and clinical privileges of physicians with exclusive contractor arrangements should terminate with the termination of the contract. Physician representatives, however, assert that, once having been granted, the medical staff membership and clinical privileges of a physician contractor should be independent of the contract and therefore continue after termination of the contract.

It is apparent that the latter condition could pose major problems for a hospital seeking to enter into an exclusive arrangement with a subsequent physician or group, particularly where the services in question require the use of hospital space, facilities, and personnel. On the other hand, members of the medical staff may wish to continue to utilize the professional services of the physician(s) whose contract has been terminated.

It is of some interest that physician managers of professional corporations that have exclusive contracts to provide specific services to hospitals and that hire physicians as employees to provide the contracted-for services have tended recently to favor contracts that condition medical staff membership and clinical privileges on the continued employment of the physician by the contracting corporation.

If a hospital and a physician or physician group agree to link medical staff membership and clinical privileges to the term of the contract, it is necessary for this to be stated in *both the contract and the medical staff bylaws*. Absence of provisions in the medical staff bylaws limiting medical staff membership and clinical privileges to the term of exclusive contract arrangements can provide a basis for physicians whose contracts have terminated to assert that their membership and privileges should continue, notwithstanding contractual terms to the contrary. This issue has been the subject of considerable, often bitter, litigation.

The necessary revisions in the medical staff bylaws require agreement by the medical staff. This is one reason it is important for the hospital to involve the medical staff in the development of strategies and policies that pertain to the provision of medical services.

Examples of terms pertaining to credentialing procedures and medical staff privileges are:

Example 1:

All physicians furnished by Corporation performing services under this Agreement shall be licensed to practice medicine in the State of _____ and shall be qualified physicians who specialize in the practice of _____. Any physician furnished by Corporation to perform services at the Hospital shall be required to qualify as a member in good standing of the professional staff of the Hospital with all the privileges and upon qualification shall be subject to all the responsibilities of such staff membership, in accordance with the Medical Staff Bylaws, Rules, and Regulations as prescribed by the Hospital. Any physician furnished by Corporation shall be subject to approval by the Medical Staff and the Board of Trustees.

Example 2:

The physicians employed by the Corporation to provide emergency medical services for the Corporation at the Hospital shall satisfy the following requirements:

1. Shall furnish proof of current licensure and registration to practice medicine in the State of _____ and certification in Basic Cardiac Life-support, Advanced Cardiac Life-support, and Advanced Trauma Life-support within two (2) years of the date of execution of this Agreement, or if a new physician employee, within one (1) year of date of hire.

2. Shall be a graduate of an approved emergency medicine program or Board Certified or Eligible. All new employed physicians shall be certified within two years of employment.

3. Shall furnish proof of current DEA number.

4. Shall be appointed by the Hospital Board of Trustees as a Member of the Medical Staff purusant to all credentialing, policies, and standards of the Medical Staff Bylaws, as may be in effect from time to time.

5. Shall observe and comply with the Medical Staff Bylaws and Department Rules and Regulations as may be in effect from time to time.

These examples do not refer to termination of clinical privileges with termination of the contract. This provision appears under the section of the agreements that sets out the conditions for termination and will be shown below.

Qualification

The agreement should list the minimum qualifications that are required of all physicians before they are allowed to provide services under the contract. The qualifications should be high enough for the hospital to ensure high-quality care for its patients, but not so high as to render contracting impossible. Qualifications commonly required are licensure; specialty certification (or eligibility for certification), including recommendations of the Joint Commission on Accreditation of Healthcare Organizations (JCAHO) and state requirements; DEA registration; and appointment to the medical staff with attendant clinical privileges.

Statements pertaining to qualifications may be combined with those that refer to medical staff credentialing and privileges, as shown in the examples in the preceding section.

Status of the Parties

Although not dispositive of the nature of the relationship being established, there should be a statement that clearly states that the parties intend their relationship to be that of independent contractors and not employer-employee. The statement should indicate that the physician is not subject to control by the hospital in rendering professional services and that the hospital is not responsible for withholding federal, state, and local taxes; Social Security contributions; etc.

In the performance of the duties and obligations devolving upon the Corporation under this Agreement, it is mutually understood and agreed that Corpo-

---

ration through its physicians and employees is at all times acting and performing as an independent contractor. The Hosptial shall neither have nor exercise any control or direction over the methods by which the Corporation or the Corporation's employees under the control and direction of the Physician shall perform their work and functions. The sole interest and responsibility of the Hospital is to ensure that the services offered by the _____Department shall be performed and rendered in a competent, efficient, and satisfactory manner. The standards of medical practice and duties of the Corporation through its Physician and employees shall be determined pursuant to the Bylaws of the Medical Staff of the Hospital. All applicable provisions of law and other rules and regulations of any and all governmental authorities relating to licensure and regulations of physicians and hospitals, and to the _____Department, shall be fully complied with by all parties hereto. In addition, the parties shall operate and conduct the _____Department in accordance with the standards and recommendations of the Joint Commission on Accreditation of Healthcare Organizations; the Code of Regulations of the Hospital; and the Bylaws, Rules and Regulations of the Medical Staff, as may be in effect from time to time.

Exclusivity

If the contracting physician or professional corporation is to have an exclusive right to provide the services described in the agreement, it is important to state this intent clearly. Exclusive contracts are becoming increasingly common for services provided in emergency departments and in radiology, anesthesiology, and pathology.

Exclusive contracts have been the subject of numerous legal challenges from excluded physicians. They allege that such agreements restrain their freedom to practice their profession and deny them their rights without due process of law. A major recent decision of the U.S. Supreme Court held that most exclusive clinical service agreements do not constitute per se violations of the federal antitrust laws. *Jefferson Parish Hospital Dist. No.2 v. Hyde*, 104 S.Ct. 1551 (1984). The majority of the Court said that a per se analysis was not applicable in the *Hyde* case because the hospital did not control a large enough share of the market to force patients to use the services of the anesthesiologists affiliated with the hospital. However, an exclusive arrangement shown to constitute an unreasonable restraint of trade or to foreclose physicians from being able to enter the market might constitute an antitrust violation. Thus, exclusive arrangements need to be justified by legitimate concerns over factors affecting patient care.

Recent court decisions have similarly tended to uphold exclusive agreements that are challenged on the basis of denial of due process. Such arrangements have been upheld as reasonable exercises of a hospital's authority to manage its facilities in the best interests of patients and the community. A physician whose clinical privileges are not affected by an exclusive arrangement has no right of procedural due process when the hospital enters into an exclusive agreement.

Representative examples of terms providing for exclusivity are:

Example 1:

The right herein granted to the Corporation to furnish physician's services to the general public in the Emergency Room of the Hospital is an exclusive right, and the Hospital shall not cause or permit the services of other physicians to be utilized therein, except for use by attending physicians for examination or treatment of their own private patients.

Example 2:

During the term of this Agreement, Corporation shall have the exclusive right to perform all medical imaging at the Hospital and any associated outpatient facilities (including, without limitation, x-ray, ultrasound, etc.) and shall provide radiology and nuclear medicine services of satisfactory quality in a competent, efficient, and satisfactory manner to both inpatients and outpatients of the Hospital. The exclusive grant of medical imaging herein contained shall not act to prevent any physician of the Hospital Medical Staff on the date hereof (other than Radiologists) from continuing to perform medical imaging to the same extent as existing on the date hereof. Further, if the attending physician or patient requires a second opinion, such opinion shall be rendered by a Radiologist of their choice. The medical imaging procedure, however, shall be the exclusive privilege of the Corporation.

Scope of Duties

The agreement should specify in as much detail as possible the contractor's duties and responsibilities. In general, the duties of contracting physicians fall within three areas: administrative duties, services to patients, and services to the hospital and medical staff.

Administrative duties include:

■ Administration of the physician's department including hiring and supervising of nonprofessional staff, establishing departmental policies and procedures, participating in the budget and long-range planning processes, and overseeing the management and planning of space, equipment, and supplies.

■ Training and supervision of nursing and technical staff.

■ Ensuring that the department satisfies all regulatory, licensure, and accreditation standards.

Services to patients include:

■ Responsibilities for patient treatment.

- Consultations with other members of the medical staff.

- Ensuring the availability of services during specified periods and whether on-site or on-call.

- Preparation of proper records and reports.

Services to the hospital and medical staff include:

- Continuing education of the medical staff.

- Participation on hospital and medical staff committees.

- Utilization review and quality assurance.

- Participation in marketing, outreach, and community relations activities.

Additional duties may include teaching obligations, research, preparation and presentation of professional papers, and grants administration.

Because in many respects the delineation of the duties of the contracting phyisician is the most important part of the agreement, considerable care and attention should be applied to drafting language that specifies as clearly as possible the intentions and expectations of the parties.

Example:

Corporation shall furnish a Board-Certified or -Eligible Radiologist who shall be acceptable to the Hospital and who shall serve as the Director of the Department of Radiology of the Hospital. In administrative relationships, the Director of the Department shall cooperate with the Administration of the Hospital in providing information regarding budgetary and other needs of the Department, in developing administrative regulations as they pertain to the Department, and in ensuring effective management of the Department.

Corporation shall operate the Department of Radiology and exercise its best efforts to provide medical management of said Department, and shall use the premises solely for the practice of Radiology. Corporation shall comply with all laws relating to clinical operations of said Department as well as the rules and regulations of Hospital accrediting bodies.

Corporation shall be available during normal working hours (7:30 a.m. until 4:00 p.m.), and on an "on-call" basis at other times, three hundred and sixty-five (365) days per year, twenty-four (24) hours per day, for consultation with any member of the Medical Staff of the Hospital regarding the well-being of patients and any and all medical or surgical matters of their mutual concern.

In the same regard, Corporation shall be available during normal working hours for consultation with Department Heads, Supervisors, and like persons with responsibility in the Hospital whenever such consultations appear necessary or advisable.

All matters pertaining to service expansion, products, or radiological services shall be regularly discussed and jointly determined by the Administrator and the Corporation and approved by the Board of Trustees of the Hospital.

The initiation and carrying on of clinical research projects and other items of conduct wherein the Department of Radiology may be involved shall be discussed and determined by Corporation and the Administrator, and approved by the Board of Trustees of the Hospital.

A second example may be found in the sample contract provided at the end of this chapter.

Outside Practice

Particularly with exclusive arrangements, the hospital may seek to limit a contracting physician's outside practice. This may be desired both to ensure the availability of the physician to provide the contracted-for services and to prevent the physician from competing with the hospital. Limitations on outside practice by independent contractors must be carefully circumscribed to avoid a finding that the physician is an employee rather than an independent contractor.

A hospital may limit a contracting physician from practicing outside the contract by limiting the use of its own facilities for treatment of private practice patients or by prohibiting the physician from practicing in an outside facility that competes with the hospital.

Restrictions on activities of contracting physicians or on practice outside the hospital should be specific and reasonable with respect to time, place, and the nature of the activities that are prohibited.

Covenants not to compete during or after the term of the agreement should be consistent with the law and judicial decisions of the jurisdiction in which the hospital is located. Such covenants will generally be upheld if they are ancillary or incidental to a lawful contract, are supported by adequate consideration, are reasonable with respect to the parties and the public, and impose only such restraint upon the physician as is necessary to protect the hospital's interests. Some states, however, prohibit limitations on a physician's practice after termination of a contract.

Example:

The Corporation shall not contract for services for any other Hospital Emergency Department or Urgent Care Center other than one affiliated with the Hospital within the geographic service area of the Hospital while this Agreement is in effect. The Corporation agrees that it shall not permit nor retain as a full- time employee any physician offering services to a Hospital Emergency Department or Urgent Care Center within the geographic service area of the Hospital. Notwithstanding the foregoing, employees who may be employed by a Hospital Emergency Room or Urgent Care Center within the geographic service area of the Hospital may be employed part-time by the Corporation as needed upon approval by the Hospital, which approval shall not be unreasonably withheld.

Professional Expenses

The contract should specify whether any professional expenses incurred by the contracting physician will be reimbursed by the hospital.

Example:

The Corporation shall be solely responsible for all personal and professional expenses incurred by its employees in rendering services under this Agreement, including, but not limited to, licensing and registration fees, professional liability insurance, membership fees and dues of professional societies and organizations, medical books and journals, and expenses incurred in attending coventions, meetings, and continuing education programs.

Professional Liability Insurance Coverage

The agreement should require that the contracting physician be covered by a professional liability insurance policy. The terms should specify (1) the minimum amount of coverage that is required, (2) that coverage includes all of the contractor's associated physicians and employees, and (3) that the contractor will provide the hospital with a copy of the insurance policy or cause the insurer to provide the hospital with a current certificate of insurance. The agreement should also require the physician to notify the hospital in advance of any alteration or cancellation of the policy.

Where possible, the policy should cover all negligent acts that occur during the coverage period ("occurrence" policy) rather than claims made during the term of the policy ("claims-made" policy). If it is not possible to obtain an occurrence policy, the agreement should require the physician to purchase a "tail" policy to cover claims that may be brought for alleged negligent acts that occurred during the term of the contract.

The agreement should also require the hospital to purchase and maintain professional liability, general liability, fire, and extended coverage insurance and to provide the contracting physician with proof of the existence of these policies.

Example:

Corporation shall maintain in force and effect at all times professional liability insurance in the amount of _____ million dollars per occurrence, _____million dollars in the aggregate with the Hospital and its Trustees as named insured, as their interest may appear, in a form acceptable to the Hospital. Further, said policy shall contain provisions for adequate tail insurance for those occurrences when this Agreement was in force and effect as approved by the Hospital. Proof of insurance as approved by the Hospital shall be submitted as required by the Medical Staff Bylaws and Rules and Regulations. Corporation shall furnish evidence of said insurances. Corporation agrees that it shall pay all premiums promptly and that it will notify the Hospital if any premiums payment is delinquent and thereby authorizes the Hospital to make such payments, said payment to be repaid within fourteen (14) days, along with interest at prime plus 2%. Failure to repay the Hospital for delinquent payment shall be cause to terminate this Agreement upon sixty (60) days' notice to the Corporation._

_Hospital will at all times during the term of this Agreement maintain necessary professional liability, public liability, fire and extended coverage insurance which shall have a minimum coverage of_____per occurrence/_____ _annual aggregate. Hospital agrees that it will provide the Corporation with a certificate or certificates validating the effective existence and terms of said policy of insurance._

Both Hospital and the Corporation agree that they shall be responsible for notifying their respective insurance companies of the terms of this Agreement.

Space, Supplies, and Equipment

The contract should describe the space the contracting physician will utilize and should specify:

- Location and size.

- The party having responsiblity for maintenance and repairs.

- Restrictions, if any, on the space's use.

- Provisions for alterations and expansions.

- The terms of any lease arrangements.

- The rights of the parties if the premises are destroyed or if services are otherwise interrupted.

The agreement should also specify which supplies are to be provided by the hospital and which by the physician, the responsibilities of each party for maintaining records for cost and control purposes, and standards for the quantity and quality of items used in patient care.

Additionally, the agreement should specify the party having responsibility for the ownership, use, control, inspection, maintenance, repair, and replacement of capital equipment to be used by the contracting physician. The contract should also provide for consultation on the need for new equipment.

Example 1:

The Hospital has agreed to make available exclusively to Corporation the space designated by the Hospital and any associated outpatient facility for the Department of Radiology. In addition, the Hospital shall make available, upon the request of Corporation, such equipment and supplies for the proper operation and conduct of said Department as mutually agreed upon by the Hospital and Corporation. The Hospital shall also keep and maintain said equipment in good order and repair. The Hospital shall furnish the Department of Radiology with utilities and with such ordinary housekeeping, laundry, and other services that may be required for the proper operation and conduct of said Department. Corporation shall submit all requisitions for supplies and new equipment through regular Hospital channels.

Example 2:

The Hospital shall provide space, equipment, supplies, and personnel to assist the Department in providing high-quality emergency services to the Hospital's patients as required by the JCAHO and in compliance with all federal, state and local laws, regulations and ordinances. Space, equipment, and supplies shall be supplied pursuant to the fiscal and budget policies of the Hospital. The Corporation shall submit its recommendations for the Department pursuant to said policies and procedures and Corporation agrees that final proof for recommendations and requests are made by the Hospital's Board of Trustees. The Hospital shall be responsible for ownership, inspection, control, maintenance, and repair and replacement of and service contracts for all equipment used in the provision of emergency services.

Support Personnel

The contract should state which party will hire and pay nonprofessional personnel in the service or department of the contracting physician. The agreement should also provide for consultation and review concerning the number of employees and their qualifications and standards of performance.

If nonphysician personnel are supplied by the hospital, the agreement should indicate whether or not they are hospital employees entitled to the same benefits as other hospital employees and what role, if any, the contracting physician has in their hiring and supervision. If such personnel are supplied by the contracting physician or corporation, the agreement should require that they are bound by all applicable hospital rules and regulations.

Example:

Except as pertains to professional personnel, all personnel required for the proper operation of the Department of Radiology shall be employed or assigned by the Hospital. The selection and retention of personnel shall be subject to the review of the Director of Radiology and the Administrator. Except as pertains to professional personnel, salaries, benefits, and personnel policies applicable to persons employed in the Department of Radiology shall conform to general Hospital policies governing employees in similar personnel classifications. The Hospital agrees to consult with the Director of Radiology on the number and necessary qualifications of personnel assigned to assist in the provision of the Department's services. The Hospital shall also provide one qualified individual to act as lay administrator of the Department who, in consultation with the Director of Radiology, shall conduct the administrative affairs of the Department.

Physician Recruitment and Hiring

Agreements, particularly those with physician groups or corporations, should set out restrictions and requirements for the hiring of associate physicians. The terms should address the qualifications and credentials of the physicians and require that they be eligible for medical staff membership and hospital privileges. The agreement should subject all physicians employed by the contractor to the medical staff bylaws, rules, and regulations. Additionally, there should be a remedy for failure to comply with the bylaws, rules, and regulations and provisions allowing the hospital to request or demand termination of an associate physician for specified reasons, such as unsatisfactory performance or conduct.

An important term is one that links medical staff membership and clinical privileges to continued employment by the contracting group or corporation and provides for acknowledgement by the employed physician of the independent contractor that clinical privileges cease with termination of employment with the contractor.

Example:

The Corporation shall provide and assign its physicians to render services at the Hospital pursuant to Medical Staff Bylaws and Departmental Rules and Regulations. Physicians employed by the Corporation shall be answerable to the Corporation.

Physicians employed by the Corporation shall be appointed by the Hospital's Board of Trustees as members of the Medical Staff pursuant to all Credentialing Policies and Standards of the Medical Staff Bylaws.

Medical Staff membership and the right to provide service in the Department shall terminate automatically, immediately, and without notice at the time the physician is no longer an employee of the Corporation.

Corporation shall provide to Hospital an original signed statement by each

---

physician employee or independent contractor certifying that he or she now meets and will continue in the future to meet the requirements for licensure, the necessary certification for providing services within the Department, and continued exercise of clinical privileges, and acknowledging his or her staff privileges shall terminate upon termination of employment with Corporation.

Compensation

There are a number of alternative compensation arrangements that may be used by the physician and the hospital. Major factors affecting the choice of arrangement are the regulations affecting reimbursement from Medicare, the Medicare and Medicaid Fraud and Abuse Amendments, and state laws affecting particular systems of reimbursement.

Alternative compensation arrangements include:

■ Payment by the hospital of a fixed fee for administrative and professional services.

■ Payment by the hospital of a fixed fee for administrative services, with the physician billing separately for professional services.

■ Guarantee by the hospital of a minimum gross income for the physician.

■ Payment by the hospital of a specified percentage of the gross charges or net receipts attributable to the physician's services.

■ Fee-for-service.

■ Physician-leased department.

Each arrangement has advantages and disadvantages regarding reimbursement, control, and incentives for productivity, efficiency, and cost control by the physician. For example, while fixed fee arrangements are relatively simple, they represent a fixed cost to the hospital and may lead courts to conclude that the physician is an employee rather than an independent contractor.

Payment of a percentage of gross charges or net receipts provides an incentive to the physician contractor to control costs. However, such arrangements may be challenged as fee-splitting devices prohibited by state law. Additionally, unless carefully drafted, they may risk violating the prohibitions against fraud and abuse contained in the Medicare and Medicaid statutes.

Because each arrangment involves a multiplicity of legal, regulatory, and accounting consequences for both parties, selection of a particular arrangement should be made only after a careful analysis by legal and accounting consultants.

Example:

Corporation shall be solely responsible for billing, collecting, and other administrative processes regarding such fees, charges, and entitlements, and for determining the amounts thereof. Corporation agrees that the amounts of said fees, charges, and entitlements shall be consistent with the customary rates for similar services rendered in private, nonprofit hospitals in the metropolitan area and shall prepare a schedule of such fees, charges, and entitlements, subject to the approval of Hospital, which approval shall not be unreasonably withheld.

Hospital shall receive, own, and be entitled to all fees and charges and other monies for all Hospital services. Hospital shall be responsible for billing and collection and all administrative processes regarding such fees and charges for services rendered by Hospital. Hospital agrees that all fees, charges, and entitlements for its services shall be consistent with the rates for similar services rendered in private, nonprofit hospitals in the metropolitan area. The schedule of such hospital services shall be made available to Corporation.

Hospital and Corporation will, without charge to either party, upon request and in a timely fashion, provide pertinent billing information to assist each party in its responsibility for collection of monies due for services rendered.

Additional Charge Issues

The hospital may wish to ensure that the contracting physician or corporation conform with the hospital's traditions of providing free or discounted care to hospital employees, students, volunteers, and indigent patients.

Example 1:

Corporation agrees to provide emergency services for employees of the Hospital and nursing students of the Hospital School of Practical Nursing when such employees are injured or become ill while on duty and the Employee Health Division is not open or cannot provide the required care. Services will be rendered at no cost to the employee or Hospital. If there are third-party sources of reimbursement or Workers' Compensation coverage for such emergency physician services provided to employees or students, Corporation may bill and collect from those third-party sources.

Example 2:

The Hospital's policy of free service and comity discounts will apply to services rendered in the Emergency Room to employees, students, volunteers, clinic patients, and other persons certified by the Administrator as having a special relationship to the Hospital under established policies of the Hospital and including persons injured or becoming ill while on Hospital premises, and persons determined by the Hospital as being unable to pay for health care.

Term and Termination

The duration of the contract should be clearly specified by stating the dates that mark the beginning and end of the contract period. Ordinarily, the contract should not set a term longer than five years. Because of changing conditions, such as rules affecting reimbursement and competition from other entities or for internal management and strategy reasons, the hospital may wish to have the agreement reviewed annually before renewing it. Alternatively, the agreement may call for an initial term of one or two years with automatic renewal unless either party gives notice of a desire to terminate.

If the contract includes use by the contracting physician of facilities or equipment created or acquired with the proceeds of tax-exempt financings, certain provisions set forth by the IRS in Revenue Procedure 82-15 (1981-1 C.B. 460) must be followed to avoid a finding by the IRS that the facilities or equipment were used in the trade or business of nonexempt persons. Such a finding could lead to the loss of tax exemption on the interest paid on bonds. For example, if the contract provides for compensation of the physican on a percentage of the fees charged for services rendered by the physician, then the contract may not exceed a term of two years and the hospital must be able to terminate the contract without cause on 90 days' written notice to the physician.

Example:

The Hospital hereby contracts with the Corporation for the exclusive management and operation of the Emergency Department for a term of two (2) years commencing on _____ . Unless written notice of cancellation of this Agreement is given by one party to the other at least ninety (90) days prior to the end of the term hereof, this Agreement shall continue in full force and effect for an additonal term of two years beginning on the Anniversary date of the first term hereof. In the event that written notice of cancellation is given, termination of the Agreement shall be effective as of the final date of the existing term hereof.

Notwithstanding the above-mentioned term, it is especially understood that this Agreement terminates pursuant to Section _____ of this Agreement upon the death, incapacity, or suspension of license of the Physician. In the event of such termination, Hospital agrees to pay any and all compensation due to the Corporation to the date of termination.

The termination provision provides the parties a way out of the agreement in case of conflicts, failures of performance, or other events. This provision has two important legal implications. First, it allows either party to end the relationship subject to provisions of the contract and damages for failure to perform. Second, it is evidence of the type of contractual relationship intended by the parties. Contracts that are terminable at the will of the employer are generally considered by courts to be employer-employee arrangements. Contracts that require the terminating party to notify the other party of specific causes for termination are usually interpreted as independent contractor agreements.

Contracts should allow for termination for no cause, upon written notice in advance to the other party, or for specified causes that are listed in the agreement. Examples of causes that may lead to termination are loss of licensure, medical staff membership, or clinical privileges on the part of the physician, or loss of accreditation or provider status under Medicare on the part of the hospital.

A potential disadvantage of listing causes is that if one party's conduct is unsatisfactory but is not a listed cause, a termination for cause is not sanctioned under the agreement. For this reason, any listing of causes should be exhaustive but should be confined to matters that are essential to the agreement.

It is useful for the contract to afford a party that is breaching the agreement an opportunity to correct the breach within a reasonable time after being notified of the breach.

The right of the contracting physician to continue medical staff membership and clinical privileges after termination of the agreement should be specified. Ordinarily, hospitals will want to provide that termination of exclusive arrangements for any reason will lead to automatic termination of medical staff membership and clinical privileges that are linked to the performance of the physician's duties under the agreement without recourse to the fair hearing and appeals procedures otherwise available under the medical staff bylaws.

It is common for hospitals to request from each physician rendering services under the contract a written, signed statement acknowledging that medical staff membership and clinical privileges terminate automatically upon termination of the agreement and stating that, upon termination of the contract, the physician waives all rights to the fair hearing and appeals procedures that are available under the medical staff bylaws. It is important that the medical staff bylaws explicitly provide for such automatic termination of membership and privileges and waiver of due process rights in the case of contracting physicians.

Example:

Corporation may terminate this Agreement for true economic hardship (defined for this purpose as an anticipated loss of more than _____ during the initial twelve (12) months of this Agreement) upon ninety (90) days' written notice to the Hospital at any time within the first twelve (12) months of this Agreement.

Hospital or Corporation may terminate this Agreement immediately upon written notice by registered mail to the other party in the event that:

1) Corporation or Hospital is liquidated or dissolved or upon assignment of this Agreement by Corporation or Hospital without the other party's written consent.

2) Corporation or Hospital fails to obtain or maintain the required insurance as provided herein.

3) Any of the personnel as set forth on Schedule A hereof for whatever reason ceases to be in the employer Corporation, to be insurable, to be licensed as required by this Agreement, or to be a member in good standing of the Medical Staff of Hospital, provided that Corporation is unable to replace such physician or physician on said Schedule A with another physician as provided under Article _____ ,herein.

4) It is expressly agreed that continuation of this Agreement is dependent upon the Physician's continued membership on the Medical Staff of the Hospital and that this Agreement shall be terminated in the event that Physician's clinical privileges are revoked, which termination shall be effective on the date that such privileges have been revoked.

5) In the event Physician's license, certification, or registration is revoked or suspended, this Agreement shall be terminated, which termination shall be effective as of the date of such revocation or suspension.

Termination of this Agreement, for whatever reason, will result in the automatic loss of clinical privileges and Medical Staff membership of the Corporation's physicians and its employees, without the right to recourse to the fair hearing and appeals procedure as provided by the Medical Staff Bylaws.

Access to Books and Records

The agreement should specify the contractor's obligation to generate and maintain medical records and reports and business or financial records and reports. Medical records and reports should be in a form that is consistent with the hospital's regulations affecting medical records and with the requirements of accrediting agencies.

Federal law (Omnibus Reconciliation Act of 1980, Section 952) requires contractors and related subcontractors providing services with a value or cost of $10,000 or more during any 12-month period to agree in writing to allow certain governmental officials access to all pertinent books and records. Access must be allowed for a period of four years following the date on which the services were provided. An example of a clause providing access to books and records appears in the agreement at the end of this chapter.

TEFRA Requirements; Allocation Agreements and Documentation

Agreements with all physicians who provide services that are reimbursable under Part A of the Medicare program must specify the amount of time the physician will spend on Part A and on Part B services. Time records or other documentation must be available to verify this allocation of time. Failure to execute a written allocation agreement will result in 100 percent of the physician's time being considered Part B services. This will prevent the hospital from receiving any Part A reimbursement for compensation paid to the physician and preclude both the hospital and the physician from obtaining Part B reimbursement if the criteria set forth in the regulations for such reimbursement are not met.

Daily time records must be kept by the physician and retained for four years after rendering the services. It is suggested that legal counsel having expertise with Medicare regulations be consulted for appropriate language for allocation agreements.

Disputes

It is recommended that the agreement provide a mechanism for resolving disputes that offers an alternative to litigation.

Example:

If a dispute should arise between the Hospital and the Corporation with respect to their obligations under, or the interpretation of, this Agreement, either the Hospital or the Corporation may demand that the dispute be settled by arbitration before a single arbitrator in accordance with the rules of the American Arbitration Association. The award of the Arbitrator shall be final and binding. This procedure shall be the exclusive means of settling any disputes that may arise under this Agreement.

Changes in the Law

Because the laws and regulations that affect medical practice, hospital management, and reimbursement are subject to frequent and substantial changes, it is advisable that the contract allow a party that is seriously and adversely affected by a change in law or regulation to demand a renegotiation of the contract or to terminate the agreement if satisfactory revisions in it cannot be made.

Nonassignability

Because physicians' services are personal and subject to medical staff bylaws, rules, and regulations, it is advisable that the contracting physician or corporation not be allowed to assign the agreement to another party. Alternatively, the agreement may allow for assignment of the contract by one party with the written approval of the other party. An exception to the nonassignability provision may permit assignment by the hospital in the event of reorganization, merger, or bankruptcy to any successor entity operating the facility now operated by the hospital.

Miscellaneous

Contracts ordinarily have a number of standard terms that pertain to the execution of the agreement. These terms are:

1. Notice--stating the manner and form of notices that are required to be given under the contract and the name, title, and address of the person to whom notices are to be sent.

2. Integration Clause--indicating that the agreement integrates and supercedes all previous agreements between the parties with respect to the subject matter of the agreement and constitutes the entire agreement between the parties.

3. Governing Law--declaring that the agreement has been executed in accordance with the laws of the state and will be construed and enforced in accordance with the state's laws.

At the end of the contract, space is provided for the names, titles, addresses, and signatures of the principals signing for each party, and for the date of the signing.

Employment Agreement

Many sections of the employment agreement are similar to those described above for the independent contractor agreement. This discussion will indicate those sections that require language appropriate or necessary for an employment agreement and those sections in which language can be used that is similar to the independent contractor agreement.

Heading

Same as for independent contractor agreement.

Recitals

These are similar to those in the independent contractor agreement, except that it may not be necessary to state any business justifications if an exclusive arrangement is not contemplated.

Definitions

Same as for independent contractor agreement.

Appointment

This term may be similar to the independent contractor agreement except that the employment agreement should clearly state that the hospital is employing the physician.

Qualifications

Same as for independent contractor agreement.

Status of the Parties

It should be clearly stated the physician is an employee of the hospital. This can be stated in the section on Appointment and may not require a separate section.

Exclusivity

This provision is usually not necessary, because employment arrangements do not generally create exclusive relationships.

Medical Staff Privileges

This section can be similar to that in the independent contractor agreement. However, because employment arrangements are not generally exclusive arrangements, it may not be necessary to link termination of medical staff membership and clinical privileges to termination of employment.

Scope of Duties

This section is similar to that in the independent contractor agreement. A key difference is that the employment agreement should clearly state that the employed physician is under the direction of the administrator of the hospital or his or her designees and is expected to perform additional duties that may be assigned. Additionally, the agreement should state that the employed physician is neither the employer of other physicians in the department nor at financial risk for their services in any way. The employed physician serving as head of a department may want the contract to specify that he or she shall be consulted if additional physicians in the department are employed by the hospital.

Outside Practice

This section may be similar to that in the independent contractor agreement. Ordinarily, the hospital will want to forbid any practice by the employed physician outside the hospital. At the least, the hospital may require that practice outside the hospital not be permitted without the written approval of the administrator.

Employed physicians whose contracts provide that premiums for professional liability insurance are paid by the hospital should determine that the terms of the policy cover activities conducted outside the hospital. Otherwise, such activities may not be insured or the physician will be responsible for obtaining a separate professional liability policy.

Professional Expenses

The contract should state what, if any, professional expenses will be paid by the hospital and indicate if there is a maximum amount that the hospital will pay.

Professional Liability Insurance Coverage

Ordinarily, the hospital's own insurance policy will cover services provided by employed physicians. Where this is so, this section may either be omitted or simply state this fact. If liability coverage for professional services is not included in the hospital's policy, it is necessary to draft language similar to that found in the independent contractor agreement.

Space, Supplies, and Equipment

This section should specify the space, supplies, and equipment the hospital will provide the physician. Ordinarily, an employed physician will not be responsible for the maintenance and repair of equipment or the furnishing of supplies. It is reasonable, therefore, for the hospital to stipulate that the space, supplies, and equipment are to be used only for hospital purposes.

Support Personnel

Employed physicians will not ordinarily be expected to hire and pay for non-professional personnel. Therefore, this section can be omitted. If the physician is expected to supervise nonprofessional personnel, this should be stated in the section on "Scope of Duties."

Physician Recruitment and Hiring

As with nonprofessional personnel, employed physicians will not be hiring and paying for additional physicians in the department. If the physician is employed as the director of a department, the contract should provide for consultation by the hospital administrator before the hospital hires additional physicians for that department.

Compensation

The most common compensation arrangement for employed physicians is straight salary. The contract should specify the fringe benefits that will be provided or, if applicable, state that fringe benefits will be the same as for other hospital employees.

Any other compensation arrangement that is used should be described in detail.

Additional Charge Issues

Same as for the independent contractor agreement if the employed physician is not salaried for Medicare Part B services to patients.

Term and Termination

This section should be similar to that in the independent contractor agreement. Because the hospital is liable for the actions of employed physicians, the contract should provide the hospital with a right for immediate termination for specified causes or for termination upon short notice.

Access to Books and Records

This section is not required in an employment agreement because the books and records of the employed physician are the property of the hospital.

TEFRA Requirements; Allocation Agreements and Documentation

Same as for the independent contractor agreement.

Disputes

Same as for the independent contractor agreement.

Changes in the Law

Because the hospital is the only party that could be harmed by changes in the laws or regulations affecting hospital management or reimbursement, employed physicians cannot be expected to agree to this section. It can and probably should be omitted.

Nonassignability

This section is not applicable to employment agreements.

Miscellaneous

Same as for the independent contractor agreement.

Sample Agreement

The agreement reproduced below is a contract for Emergency Department services to be provided by an independent contractor. It is presented to illustrate many of the points discussed in this chapter. It is not intended, however, to provide "ideal" language. There is no such thing as ideal language. Rather, as stated at the outset, the language that is adopted should reflect and enable the parties to achieve their respective needs and goals.

Agreement For Emergency Care Services

THIS AGREEMENT is made and entered into this ___ day of ____, 1985, by and between _____ HOSPITAL, INC., hereinafter referred to as "Hospital," and ____ INC., hereinafter referred to as "Corporation," a professional corporation.

Recitals

Whereas, the Hospital is a not-for-profit Corporation that owns and operates a hospital in _____, in which is located an Emergency Department.

Whereas, the Corporation is a professional corporation created and existing purusant to the laws of the State of _____ and doing business in the State of ___.

Whereas, as a full service acute care hospital, the Hospital provides emergency care services for the community through the Emergency Department. The Hospital has determined that the Emergency Department can be administered most efficiently and operated most effectively by one medical professional corporation. The Hospital has determined that effective delivery of emergency care services requires the management and marketing of such services with particular attention to the interests of the community served by the Hospital, the provision and improvement of the quality of patient care by the proper staffing of physicians, the establishment and monitoring of professional performance to ensure high-quality care for all patients, the provision of continuous professional services, the controlling of costs, the provision of professional service to all patients in a timely manner, the provision of effective and efficient medical audit and professional review procedures, the representation of Hospital in the _____ County emergency medical system and the insistence on improved medical education in emergency medicine.

Whereas, the Hospital has further determined that the foregoing goals may be met most effectively and the emergency department may be administered most efficiently by a professional medical corporation headed by a physician with experience and training in the field of emergency medicine.

Whereas, the Corporation has retained the services of _____, MD, as its President and Chief Operating Officer, hereinafter referred to as "Physician," duly licensed by the State of ____ Board of Medical Examiners and registered as a physician and Board Certified in Emergency Medicine pursuant to the laws of the State of ____.

Whereas, the Parties recognize that certain services and facilities (as hereinafter stated) will be provided to the Corporation by the Hospital in order to (i) realize economies resulting from the use of better purchasing arrangements and general administrative expertise of the Hospital, and (ii) relieve the Corporation of the nonmedical demands placed upon professional time in connection with such services and facilities. It is the expectation of the Parties that this practice will benefit patients by reducing health care costs and increase the quality of professional service.

NOW, THEREFORE, in consideration of the mutual promises and covenants contained herein, the parties agree as follows:

I. APPOINTMENT APPROVAL

A. This contract shall be in effect and binding upon the Parties upon appointment of Physician as Director of the Emergency Department, as approved by the Hospital's Board of Trustees pursuant to all requirements of the Hospital's Medical Staff By-Laws and execution of this contract by both Parties hereto.

B. The Corporation has the exclusive right to control and perform all physician services rendered at said Emergency Department of Hospital. Said exclusive right shall recognize legitimate and timely requests for treatment of private patients by said patient's personal physicians.

C. In accordance with the provisions of paragraph (B) of this Article above, as well as in the event of treatment by noncorporate physicians as set forth in paragraph (B) of this Article above, the Corporation shall have no legal responsibility for any services performed in the Emergency Department by any personnel other than those persons employed and provided by the Corporation.

D. In accordance with the provisions of paragraph (B) of this Article, Hospital shall have no legal responsibility for services rendered in the Emergency Department by the Director or physicians provided by the Corporation.

E. The Corporation and Hospital agree that no services other than emergency medical services shall be rendered in said Emergency Department of hospital. Corporation specifically agrees that the personnel provided by Corporation hereunder shall practice their professions of medicine and specialization within the said Emergency Department in full compliance with approved methods and practices of such professional specialty. Corporation's physicians shall not engage in the private practice of medicine at the Hospital as a result of this exclusive Agreement and shall not be entitled to admitting privileges at the Hospital.

F. The said Emergency Department shall operate as a medical care unit for the benefit of the persons and patients coming to the Hospital for services.

II. TERM

A. The Hospital hereby contracts with the Corporation for the exclusive management and operation of the Emergency Department for a term of three (3) years commencing on _____. Unless written notice of cancellation of this Agreement is given by either party to the other at least ninety (90) days prior to the end of the term hereof, this Agreement shall continue in full force and effect for an additional term of three years beginning on the Anniversary date of the first term hereof. In the event such written notice of cancellation is given, termination of the Agreement shall be effective as of the final date of the existing term hereof.

B. The Corporation hereby accepts such engagement and agrees to operate the Department according to the terms and conditions contained in this Agreement. Notwithstanding the abovementioned term, it is expressly understood that this Agreement terminates pursuant to Section XIX of this Agreement upon the death, incapacity, or suspension of license of the Physician. In the event of such termination, Hospital agrees to pay any and all compensation due to the Corporation to the date of termination.

III. CONFLICT OF INTEREST

A. The Corporation shall not contract for services with any other hospital emergency department or urgent care center other than one affiliated with the Hospital within the geographic service area of the Hospital while this Agreement is in force and effect. The Corporation agrees that it shall not permit nor retain as a full-time employee any physician offering his or her services to a hospital emergency department or urgent care center within the geographic service area of the Hospital. Notwithstanding the foregoing, employees who may be employed by a hospital emergency room or urgent care center within the geographic service area of the hospital may be employed part time by the Corporation as needed upon approval of the Hospital, which approval shall not be unreasonably withheld.

B. The Hospital agrees that it shall not contract with any physician, person, or business entity other than the Corporation for emergency services at the Hospital or its affiliates while this Agreement is in force and effect.

IV. INDEPENDENT CONTRACTOR STATUS

A. In the performance of the duties and obligations devolving upon the Corporation under this Agreement, it is mutually understood and agreed that Corporation through its physicians and employees is at all times acting and performing as an independent contractor. The Hospital shall neither have nor exercise any control or direction over the methods that the Corporation, or the Corporation's employees under the control and direction of the Physician, use to perform their work and functions. The sole interest and responsibility of the Hospital is to ensure that the services offered by the Emergency Department shall be performed and rendered in a competent, efficient, and satisfactory manner. The standards of medical practice and duties of the Corporation through its Physician and employee shall be determined pursuant to the By-Laws of the Medical Staff of the Hospital. All applicable provisions of law and other rules and regulations of any and all governmental authorities relating to licensure and regulations of physicians and hospitals and to the Emergency Department in accordance with the standards and recommendations of the Joint Commission on Accreditation of Healthcare Organizations, the code of Regulations of the Hospital, and the By-Laws, Rules, and Regulations of the Medical Staff, as may be in effect from time to time.

V. SELECTION AND QUALIFICATION OF PROFESSIONAL STAFF

A. The Corporation shall provide a Board Certified Emergency Medicine Physician, experienced in the administration and clinical operations of an Emergency Department, to act as Director of the Department subject to written approval by the Hospital Board of Trustees pursuant to all requirements and procedures set forth in the Hospital's Medical Staff By-Laws and as amended from time to time.

B. The Corporation shall provide and assign its physicians to render services at the Hospital pursuant to Medical Staff By-Laws and Departmental Rules and protocols and standards as developed by the Physician as may be in effect from time to time and subject to the provisions as to the minimum standards hereinafter set forth.

c. Physicians. The physicians employed by the Corporation to provide emer
gency medical services for the Corporation at the Hospital shall satisfy the following requirements:

1. Shall furnish proof of current licensure and registration to practice medicine in the State of _____ and certification in Basic Cardiac Life Support, certification in Advanced Cardiac Life Support and certification in Advanced Trauma Life Support within two (2) years of the date of execution of this Agreement, or if a new physician employee, within one (1) year of date of hire.

2. Shall be a graduate of an approved emergency medicine program or Board Certified or Eligible. All new employed physicians shall be certified within two (2) years of employment.

3. Shall furnish proof of current DEA number.

4. Shall be appointed by the Hospital Board of Trustees as a Member of the Medical Staff pursuant to all credentialing policies and standards of the Medical Staff by-Laws, as may be in effect from time to time.

5. Shall observe and comply with the Medical Staff By-Laws and Department Rules and Regulations as may be in effect from time to time.

6. Shall be an employee of or an independent contractor answerable to the Corporation. Medical Staff Membership and the right to provide service in the Department shall terminate automatically, immediately, and without notice at the time the physician is no longer an employee of the Corporation.

7. Corporation shall provide to Hospital an original signed statement by each physician employee or independent contractor, certifying that he or she now meets and will continue in the future to meet the requirements set forth in items 1 through 5 above and acknowledging that his or her staff privileges shall terminate upon termination of employment with Corporation.

D. Subject to the retention of the Corporation's current permanent staff, the target staffing for the Emergency Department shall be the Director and five (5) full-time physicians who have graduated from an approved emergency medicine program or Board Certified or Eligible should be achieved no later than _____. This provision shall be reviewed by both Parties at that time.

VI. STATUS OF PHYSICIAN DIRECTOR AND PHYSICIANS

A. In the performance of work, duties, and responsibilities to be provided by the Director and physicians, it is understood and agreed that such personnel shall at all times act and perform as employees of the Corporation.

B. The Corporation shall be responsible for all compensation to which its employees are entitled for the performance of their professional services. The Corporation will indemnify and hold the Hospital harmless from and against any and all claims by physicians for any compensation. The Corporation agrees to pay all applicable federal, state, and local income taxes, including any and all other governmental fees, taxes, or expenses levied against it. The Corporation shall idemnify and defend the Hospital in the event that any tax authority or governmental authority prosecutes the Hospital because of the Corporation's failure to submit reports or returns, make necessary payments, or maintain records.

C. In the event Physician is no longer employed by the Corporation or in the event that this Agreement is terminated, Hospital and the Corporation hereby agree that said Physician's staff appointment and privileges at the Hospital will automatically terminate. All physicians associated with or employed by the corporation providing services under this Agreement shall have their Medical Staff appointments and privileges terminate concurrent with the termination of this Agreement. Each physician employed by the Corporation to provide services hereunder shall at the time of his employment execute and deliver to the Hospital, through the Corporation, a letter stating that he or she understands and agrees to the automatic termination of his or her staff appointment and privileges upon the occurrence of either termination of employment with the Corporation or the termination of this Agreement.

VII. SERVICES TO BE PROVIDED BY CORPORATION

A. Corporation agrees to be responsible for the overall professional functioning of the emergency Department, hereinafter referred to as "Department," providing continuous, on-site, twenty-four (24) hour, seven (7) days a week, fifty-two (52) weeks a year physician service availability in an efficient and timely manner for all services required of the Department.

1. The size of said physician staff and its make-up in terms of medical specialties shall be determined by the Corporation and Hospital consistent with Corporation's obligations hereunder to staff said Emergency Department 24 hours a day, seven days a week, during the term hereof.

2. It is expressly understood and agreed between the parties hereto as a condition of the Agreement that the physician coverage to be provided by the Corporation hereunder shall be specified on Schedule A attached hereto and made a part hereof, which schedule shall list the names of the physicians who shall, during the term of this Agreement, provide the services hereunder. In the event that a physician or physicians specified on Schedule A, other than the physician identified as Director of the Department, dies, becomes disabled, ceases to be in the employ of the Corporation, is no longer insurable, or otherwise is unable to perform services hereunder for reasons outside the control of Corporation, then Corporation shall provide a qualified substitute physician within ninety (90) days. The physician or physicians so substituted shall meet all requirements and conditions as provided in this Agreement, and shall be subject to the approval of the Hospital and its Medical Staff, which approval shall not be unreasonably withheld. No other subsitutions shall be made without the agreement of the Corporation and Hospital. It is understood and agreed that there shall be no right of substitution, in any event, for the Physician selected and named as Director of the Department, unless otherwise agreed to by the Hospital.

3. In providing the services of the physician staff as set forth above, the Corporation agrees to provide the physician services of Hospital's Emergency Department in an able, efficient, and competent manner. The Corporation agrees that the services provided hereunder shall meet the standards of the American College of Surgeons, the American Medical Association, and the Joint Commission on Accreditation of Healthcare Organizations and shall be consistent with the Ethical and Religious Directive of _____ Health Care Facilities. In addition, such physicians shall, as members of the Medical Staff, abide by the By-Laws, Rules, and Regulations of the Medical Staff.

4. Schedule A shall set forth the Corporation's proposed permanent physician staff, including full-time and part-time staff, definition of provisions for emergency/disaster coverage, and unanticipated peak service situations.

B. Corporation agrees to provide a Board Certified Emergency Medicine physician, licensed and registered in the State of ___, having a current narcotics number, certified in Basic Cardiac Life Support and in Advanced Cardiac Life Support, and qualified pursuant to the Hospital's Medical Staff By-Laws and appointed by the Hospital Board of Trustees as Director of Emergency Department. Director shall be responsible for providing such services under this Agreement, including but not limited to the following duties:

1. Plans, organizes, implements, and controls a high-quality, cost-effective Department.

2. In cooperation with Division Supervisor provides an annual budget for the Department and manages and controls expenditures pursuant thereto in cooperation with the Hospital administrative budget process.

3. In cooperation with Division Supervisor provides an annual report for the Department as required by the Hospital administrative policies.

4. Monitors the quality and appropriateness of emergency care rendered by the physicians.

5. Develops and amends, as necessary to reflect state-of-the-art care, departmental protocols and standards and responsibilities for physicians.

6. Schedules adequate physician personnel to staff department for the delivery of care, taking into consideration peak demand hours as specified on Schedule A, annexed hereto and made a part hereof and as the same may be modified by Corporation with the approval of the Hospital, such approval not to be unreasonably withheld.

7. Establishes, implements, and maintains all precautions to ensure the safe provision of emergency care and shall work and consult closely with the Hosptial Safety Committee and develop regulations, rules, and policies for safety, including but not limited to the maintenance, inspection, and repair of all equipment used in providing emergency care services.

8. Ensures that continuing educational requirements for all persons having clinical privileges in emergency medicine have been adhered to.

9. Consults and works closely with the Hospital's Medical Staff and Administration to coordinate the Department's services with other services and programs offered by the Hosptial and its Medical Staff.

10. Attends regularly scheduled meetings with the Vice President of Patient Care Services.

11. Advises the Hospital Administration regarding space, personnel, and equipment needs of the Department.

12. Arranges, upon approval of the Hospital, for a well-qualified Emergency Medicine physician to assume the duties of Director when Director is absent, as consistent with the Medical Staff By-Laws, Rules, and Regulations and as approved by the Hospital Board of Trustees.

13. Administers the Department consistent with Hospital policies so that all requirements of the Joint Commission on Accreditation of Healthcare Organizations and federal, state, and local laws, regulations, and ordinances governing the Department are fully complied with as they may exist from time to time.

14. Serves on the following Hospital and Medical Staff Committees as a voting Member:

Medical Executive Committee
Chairman of the Emergency Department Committee
Chairman of the Disaster Committee

15. Represents the Hosptial as an active member in the ____ County emergency medical systems.

16. With adequate notice to the Hospital Administration and the Medical Staff, physicians shall have a maximum total of ___ weeks for vacation. Additional time shall be permitted for continuing professional education consistent with the needs of the Department.

VIII. CORPORATION CHARGES

Corporation agrees that the amounts of said fees, charges, and entitlements shall be consistent with the customary rates for similar services rendered in private nonprofit hospitals in the Greater _____ Area and, to this end, will, from time to time, prepare a schedule of such fees, charges, and entitlements, subject to the approval of Hospital, which approval shall not be unreasonably withheld. Corporation shall accept assignment as payment in full for services provided to Medicare beneficiaries.

IX. INSURANCE

A. Corporation shall maintain in force and effect at all times professional liability insurance in the minimum amount of ____ million dollars per occurrence, ____ million dollars in the aggregate with the Hospital and its Trustees as named insured, as their interest may appear, in a form acceptable to the Hospital. Further, said policy shall contain provision for adequate tail insurance for those occurrences when this Agreement was in force and effect as approved by the Hospital. Proof of insurance as approved by the Hospital shall be submitted as required by the Medical Staff By-Laws and Rules and Regulations. Corporation shall furnish evidence or said insurances. Corporation agrees that it shall pay all premiums promptly and that it will notify the Hospital if any premium payment is delinquent and hereby authorizes the Hospital to make such payments, said payment to be repaid within fourteen (14) days along with interest at prime plus two percent. Failure to repay the Hospital of delinquent payment shall be cause to terminate this Agreement upon sixty (60) days' notice to the Corporation.

B. Hospital will at all times during the term of this Agreement maintain necessary professional liability, public liability, fire, and extended coverage insurance, which shall have a minimum coverage of ____ per occurrence/____ annual aggregate. Hospital agrees that it will provide the Corporation with a certificate or certificates validating the effective existence and terms of said policy of insurance.

C. Both Hospital and the Corporation agree that they shall be responsible for notifying their respective insurance companies of the terms of this Agreement.

X. RESPONSIBILITIES OF THE CORPORATION

A. The Corporation will be responsible for all compensation to which its employees are entitled for the performance of their services and will indemnify and hold the Hospital harmless from and against any and all claims by the Corporation's employees for any compensation.

B. The Corporation will be responsible for all taxes, levies, fines or judgments as set forth and in compliance with Section VI of the Agreement.

C. Corporation shall be responsible for the billing and have the right to remuneration for all professional services rendered by it to the Hospital's patients.

D. Corporation agrees that all records, reports, and similar documents related to treatment of patients made in the normal course of operation of the Emergency Department shall be the property of Hospital. Hospital agrees that it shall preserve and maintain all such records, reports, and documents in accordance with the requirements of law and Hospital's policy and practices. This provision as to records and documents shall survive the termination of this Agreement under any and all circumstances.

XI. ACCESS TO BOOKS AND RECORDS

If the value or cost of services provided under this Agreement is $10,000 or more within a twelve-month period, then, to the extent that the cost of such services is reimbursable by Medicare to the Hospital, the physicians agree to comply with the Access to Books, Documents, and Records of Subcontractors provisions of Section 952 of the Omnibus Reconciliation Act of 1980 (P.L. 96- 499), and 42 C.F.R. Part 420, Subpart D, Section 420.300 et seq.

In accordance with these provisions, the physicians will, upon proper written request made in conformance with 42 C.F.R. Section 420.304, allow the Comptroller General of the United States, the Secretary of Health and Human Services, and their duly authorized representatives access to this Agreement and to the physicians' books, documents, and records (as defined in 42 C.F.R. Section 420.301) necessary to certify the nature and extent of costs of Medicare reimbursable services provided under this Agreement. Such access will be allowed, upon request, until the expiration of four (4) years after the Medicare reimbursable services are furnished pursuant to this Agreement. As required by the above-referenced statute and regulations, if Medicare reimbursable services provided by physicians under this Agreement are carried out by means of a subcontract with any organization "related to" physicians, as defined in 42 C.F.R. Section 420.301, and such related organization provides services the cost or value of which is $10,000 or more over a twelve-month period, then the subcontract between physicians and the related organization shall contain a clause requiring that the related organization will, until the expiration of four (4) years after the furnishing of Medicare reimbursable services pursuant to said subcontract, upon proper request made in conformance with 42 C.F.R. Section 420.304, allow the Comptroller General of the United States, the Secretary of Health and Human Services, and their duly authorized representatives access to the subcontract and to the related organization's books, documents, and records (as defined in 42 C.F.R. Section 420.301) necessary to certify the nature and extent of costs of Medicare reimbursable services provided under the subcontract.

If physicians, or any organization "related to" the physicians furnishing services provided for in this Agreement pursuant to a subcontract with physicians, are requested to disclose any books, documents, or records relevant to this Agreement for the purpose of an audit or investigation, physicians shall notify Hospital of the nature and scope of such request and shall make available to Hospital all books, documents, or records that it intends to disclose pursuant to such request.

To the extent that this provision varies from any provision required by any regulation issued under authority of Section 952 of P.L. 96-499, the provisions of said regulation, 42 C.F.R. Party 420, as amended, shall be deemed by the parties to supersede this provision and be made a part hereof by reference.

XII. RESPONSIBILITIES OF HOSPITAL

The Hospital shall provide space, equipment, supplies, and personnel to assist the Department in providing high-quality emergency services to the Hospital's patients as required by the Joint Commission on Accreditation of Healthcare Organizations and in compliance with all federal, state, and local laws, regulations, and ordinances. Space, equipment, and supplies shall be supplied pursuant to the fiscal and budget policies and procedures of the Hospital. The Corporation shall submit its recommendations for the Department pursuant to said policies and procedures, and Corporation agrees that final approval for recommendations and requests is made by the Hospital's Board of Trustees. The Hospital shall be responsible for ownership, inspection, control, maintenance, repair and replacement, and service contracts of all equipment used in the provision of emergency services.

The Hospital shall be responsive to the needs of the Department through the capital budget process and shall not unreasonably withhold capital budget requests in relation to the total Hospital needs as reflected through the capital budget process.

The Hospital shall notify the Director as far in advance as possible of any decisions or contemplated decisions or actions of Hospital that may affect the facilities and personnel provided by Hospital hereunder or that may affect the conduct of physician's services in the Emergency Department by Corporation.

Hospital will make available to Corporation copies of the Emergency Department record that it customarily provides to such physicians providing medical services in the Emergency Department. This provision as to records and documents shall survive the termination of this Agreement under any or all circumstances.

XIII. COMMUNICATIONS AND DISPUTES

In addition to the specific covenants contained elsewhere in this Agreement regarding cooperation and consultation, parties agree further:

A. Corporation and its physicians shall, at all reasonable hours, be ready to participate in personal communications, meetings, or conferences requested by appropriate members of the Hospital Medical Staff to resolve problems arising out of the medical condition or care of patients who have received services in the Emergency Department. Further, Corporation shall be available at all times for at least telephone communications and consultation with appropriate Hospital Medical Staff in emergency situations.

B. Corporation and its physicians will participate in communications, meetings, and conferences with appropriate members of the Hospital Administrative Staff during normal working hours for the purpose of resolving issues or problems arising under this Agreement.

C. Hospital shall take all reasonable steps to insure that appropriate members of its Medical Staff shall be available and shall participate in conferences with Corporation or its physicians in the same manner and circumstances as set forth in paragraph (A) of this Article.

D. Hospital shall insure that appropriate members of its Administrative Staff shall be ready to participate during normal working hours in communications, meetings, and conferences in the same manner as set forth in paragraph (B) of this Article.

E. Either party that determines that the other has materially breached this Agreement shall give immediate notice in writing to the other party of the specifics of such alleged breach. Within two business days of the receipt of such written notice by the party charged with a breach hereof, both parties shall meet personally by their appropriate representatives who shall have authority to resolve such alleged breach. During the course of the resolution of such alleged breach, this Agreement shall remain in full force and effect. In the event that no resolution is reached within ninety (90) days from the date of receipt of written notice as aforesaid by the party charged with the breach (unless the parties mutually agree to extend said ninety-day period), then this Agreement shall terminate. Nothing contained herein shall be considered a waiver by either party of its legal rights hereunder.

F. The parties recognize that there are educational requirements established by accrediting bodies of medical and health care facilities such as the American Medical Association, the American College of Emergency Physicians, and the Joint Commission on Accreditation of Healthcare Organizations. The parties agree, therefore, that they shall cooperate in participating in educational programs and teaching functions both inside and outside the Hospital as may be necessary for compliance with said accrediting agencies.

XIV. FINANCIAL CONSIDERATION

A. Corporation shall be solely responsible for billing, collecting, and other administrative processes regarding such fees, charges, and entitlements and for determining the amounts thereof. Corporation agrees that the amounts of said fees, charges, and entitlements shall be consistent with the customary rates for similar services rendered in private nonprofit hospitals in the Greater _____ area and shall prepare a schedule of such fees, charges, and entitlements, subject to the approval of Hospital, which approval shall not be unreasonably withheld.

B. Hospital shall receive, own, and be entitled to all fees and charges and other monies for all hospital services. Hospital shall be responsible for the billing and collection and all administrative processes regarding such fees and charges for services rendered by Hospital. Hospital agrees that all fees, charges, and entitlements for its services shall be consistent with the rates for similar services rendered in private, nonprofit hospitals in the Greater _____ area. The schedule of such hospital services shall be made available to Corporation.

C. Hospital and Corporation will, without charge to either party, upon request and in a timely fashion, provide pertinent billing information to assist each party in its responsibility for collection of monies due for services rendered.

D. Corporation agrees to provide emergency services for employees of Hospital and nursing students of ____ Hospital School of Practical Nursing, when such employees are injured or become ill while on duty and Employee Health Division is not open or cannot provide the required care. Such services will be rendered at no cost to the employee or Hospital. Corporation also agrees to provide emergency services for members of the clergy or members of the religious order who are employees or independent contractors of the Hospital. Such services to clergy and religious orders will be rendered at either no cost, or at such cost as may be determined by Hospital and the Corporation. If there are third-party sources of reimbursement or Workers' Compensation coverage for such emergency physicians services provided either to Hospital employees or to members of the clergy or members of religious orders, Corporation may bill and collect from those third-party sources.

XV. ASSIGNMENT

This Agreement is entered into between the Corporation and the Hospital for the sole benefit of each of them respectively and may not be assigned by either party, nor any rights claimed hereunder for any other person or persons whatsoever. Notwithstanding the mutual nonassignability of the Agreement as set forth above, it is agreed that if the Corporation is assigned pursuant to a sale or transfer of shares whereby the sole shareholder in the Corporation is divested of more than forty-nine (49) percent of his rights and interests to another physician or group of physicians, the Hospital shall have the right to approve of said assignment and may at the Hospital's sole discretion continue this Agreement with the assignee(s).

XVI. CONSTRUCTION

This Agreement shall be construed and all of the rights, powers, and liabilities of the parties hereunder shall be determined in accordance with the laws of the State of ____.

This Agreement contains the whole understanding of the parties and supersedes all prior oral or written representations and statements between the parties.

XVII. SUPERVENING LAW

The parties recognize that this Agreement at all times is subject to applicable federal, state, and local laws, including but not limited to the National Health Planning and Resource Development Act of 1974, the Social Security Act, and the Rules and Regulations and policies of the Department of Health and Human Services, all public health and safety provisions of state law and regulations, and the rules and regulations of the Health System Agency and State Health Planning and Development Agency. The parties further recognize that this Agreement shall be subject to amendments in such laws and regulations and to new legislation and implementing rules and regulations. Any provision of law that invalidates or is inconsistent with the terms of this Agreement or that would cause one or both Parties to be in violation of the law, shall be deemed to have superseded the terms of this Agreement, provided that the Parties shall exercise their best efforts to accommodate the terms and intent of this Agreement to the greatest extent possible consistent with the requirements of law.

XVIII. NOTICES

Any notices required hereunder shall be in writing and shall be deemed to have been properly given if in writing and sent by certified or registered mail, in the case of the Hospital to its Chief Executive Officer, _____ Hospital, Inc., _____ and in the case of the Corporation to _____ or at such other place as the Corporation may designate by written notice to Hospital.

XIX. TERMINATION

A. Corporation may terminate this Agreement for true economic hardship (defined for this purpose as an anticipated loss of more than _____ during the initial twelve (12) months of this Agreement) upon ninety (90) days' written notice to the Hospital at any time within the first twelve (12) months of this Agreement.

B. Hospital or Corporation may terminate this Agreement immediately upon written notice by registered mail to the other party in the event that:

1. Corporation or Hospital is liquidated or dissolved or upon assignment of this Agreement by Corporation or Hospital without the other party's written consent.

2. Corporation or Hospital fails to obtain and maintain the required insurance as provided herein.

3. Any of the personnel as set forth on Schedule A hereof for whatever reason ceases to be in the employ of Corporation, to be insurable, to be licensed as required by this Agreement, or to be a member in good standing of the Medical Staff of Hospital, provided that Corporation is unable to replace such physician or physicians on said Schedule A with another physician as provided under Article VII, paragraph (A) (2) herein.

4. It is expressly agreed that continuation of this Agreement is dependent upon the Physician's continued membership on the Medical Staff of the Hospital and that this Agreement shall be terminated in the event that Physician's clinical privileges are revoked, which termination shall be effective on the date that such privileges have been revoked.

5. In the event Physician's license certification or registration is revoked or suspended, this Agreement shall be terminated, which termination shall be effective as of the date of such revocation or suspension.

Termination of this Agreement, for whatever reason, will result in the automatic loss of clinical privileges and Medical Staff membership of the Corporation's physicians and its employees without the right to recourse to the fair hearing and appeals procedure as provided by the Medical Staff By- Laws.

Notwithstanding any provisions of the prior immediate paragraph, termination of the contract by the Hospital for reasons of clinical competency shall be subject to review by the Medico-Administrative Forum, which shall consider all facts and circumstances relating to the termination of Agreement. It is hereby agreed and understood that the Medico-Administrative Forum shall be the only forum before which these decisions shall be reviewed.

XX. TERMINATION OF PRIVILEGES

Notwithstanding any provisions of the By-Laws, Rules and Regulations, and policies of the Hospital and of its Medical Staff, the Medical Staff membership and clinical privileges of the Physician shall terminate simultaneously with the termination of this Agreement. Provisions of said By-Laws, Rules and Regulations, and policies of the Hospital and its Medical Staff with respect to fair hearings and appellate review shall not apply.

IN WITNESS WHEREOF, the parties have executed two copies of this Agreement on the date first above written.

HOSPITAL   CORPORATION

_____, INC.   _____, INC.

By:_____   By:_____
　President and   President
　Chief Executive Officer

And   And

By:_____   By:_____
　　Secretary   Secretary

CHAPTER 4

THE HMO MEDICAL DIRECTOR'S ROLE IN CONTRACT NEGOTIATIONS

James B. Couch, M.D., J.D.

James B. Couch, MD, JD, is a physician, attorney, and medical management consultant in quality assessment, utilization management, risk management, physician credentialing, severity indexing systems, and cost-effective clinical decision-making. He has directed, researched, and taught in these areas at Hahnemann University and the University of Pennsylvania in Philadelphia. He received his doctor of jurisprudence degree from Indiana University and his medical degree from the University of Pennsylvania. He has also completed coursework toward the master of science degree in health policy and management from New York University. He practices medicine part-time at Maxicare of Philadelphia and law part-time at Nash and Company, a Pittsburgh health law firm. Dr. Couch is a member of the Liaison Council of the American Academy of Medical Directors, with a special role between the Academy and the Joint Commission on Accreditation of Hospitals on its quality of care initiative, "Agenda for Change."

Health maintenance organizations (HMOs) have a considerably longer history in this country than many physicians realize. The beginnings date to the early 1930s with the Kaiser Permanente and Ross Loos Plans. These plans grew to varying degrees at different times during the '40s and '50s, although fee for service clearly remained the dominant form of health care delivery.

One of the early entrants in the next wave of HMOs was the Harvard Community Health Plan in the late '60s. Although not owned by Harvard University, virtually all of its participating physicians have teaching appointments at the Harvard Medical School. The plan has flourished over the past two decades. It has over 300,000 subscribers in an area where fee-for-service medicine has very strong underpinnings. The plan is an example of a not-for-profit HMO, which has enjoyed steady growth in a local market, dominated by fee-for-service practitioners.

The most recent wave of HMOs has been marked by the growth of the for-profit HMO management company chains, including those spawned by insurance companies and insurer/provider joint ventures. For the most part, these chains (Maxicare, U.S. Health Care, United Health Care, etc.), insurance company plans (CIGNA Health Plan, Prudential, Metropolitan, Blue Cross/Blue Shield, etc.), and insurer/provider joint ventures (the VHA/Aetna Partners' National Health Care Plan and the HCA/Equitable Equicor Plans) should come to dominate at least the alternative delivery and possibly the entire medical practice landscape for the rest of this century.

Different HMO Models

HMOs may be categorized into one of four models[1]:

Staff Model

A broad range of primary and ancillary and certain types of specialty care are provided out of one or more centralized medical centers. The physicians are employed by the HMO and are paid a fixed salary. These HMOs often have the greatest ability to control physician practice styles, as the physician is an employee of the HMO, not an independent contractor.

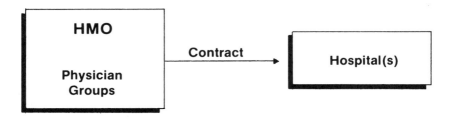

Figure 1. Staff Model

Medical Group Model

As in the staff model, care is provided out of one or more centralized medical centers where a broad range of primary and ancillary and certain types of specialty care is provided. The difference from the staff model is that medical groups contract with the HMO to deliver services only to HMO enrollees. Although the physician groups are entities separate from the HMOs, many of the HMOs are controlled by these medical groups.

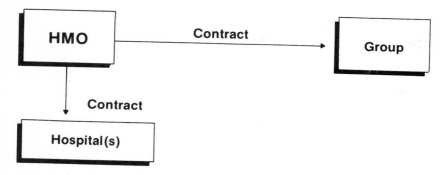

Figure 2. Medical Group Model

Individual Practice Association (IPA) Model

In an IPA, physicians and other health care providers maintain individual offices, and most of them continue to receive the majority of their business from non-HMO patients under a traditional fee-for-service arrangement. The HMO contracts with the IPA to provide services for its members, and the IPA contracts with the participating physicians to deliver the services.

The IPA is a rather loose grouping of physicians in comparison to other HMO models. IPA physicians can be in solo practice or can participate in groups. IPAs often have substantial market appeal, because they offer patients a greater choice of physicians or, perhaps, the opportunity to continue an existing physician relationship.

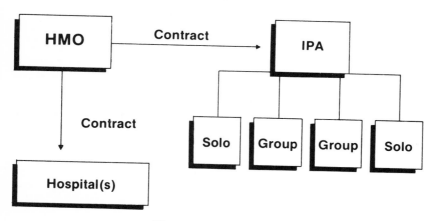

Figure 3. IPA Model

Network Model

As in the IPA model, physicians and other health care providers maintain individual offices and most continue under a fee-for-service arrangement.

However, the difference from the IPA is that the HMO contracts directly with several group practices and/or individual physicians to provide health care services to HMO enrollees.

Health Maintenance Organization Contracts with Physicians and Hospitals

Depending on the context, HMOs may take on the attributes of either a provider or a purchaser of health care services. In the physician and hospital contracting area, HMOs function as providers when they strive to compete with other HMOs, Preferred Provider Organizations (PPOs), and other providers for coveted inclusion on the lists of employers' and labor unions' health insurance benefit plans. On the other hand, HMOs function as purchasers of health care services when they, in turn, solicit competitive bids from hospitals and physicians. The ultimate goal in either role is for the HMO to negotiate the "best deal" to optimize the quality and cost- effectiveness of health care delivery to subscribers. It is this basic goal to which HMO medical directors should address themselves continually throughout the contracting process.

HMO medical directors should play a key role in negotiating with fourth-party payers (corporations, labor unions, etc.) for inclusion on their lists of "approved health insurance benefit plans." Most of these negotiations should proceed between the HMO's executive director and the director or vice president of compensation and benefits of the fourth-party payor. The following represents a nonexhaustive list of the important issues that can and generally will be handled by a nonphysician executive director:

■ Payment methods from the fourth-party payer to the HMO, including lump sums; straight capitated amounts per subscriber; partial payments of the above, with the amount of the balance tied to utilization performance of the HMO; different payment amounts, depending on the type and range of services provided to subscribers (e.g., medical, surgical, pediatric, obstetrical, mental health, dental, etc.); and different amounts tied to the overall costs of administering the program.

■ Amount of coinsurance, deductible, or copayment to be charged subscribers.

■ Methods for choosing particular providers.

■ Accessibility of services available to particular geographically localized groups of subscribers.

■ "Out of plan" coverage.

■ Ancillary services coverage.

■ Inpatient coverage, conditions, and limitations.

- "Stop loss" provisions.

- Catastrophic illness provisions.

- Extent of family and dependents' coverage.

The foregoing issues have been reasonably "cut and dried" in the past in negotiations between nonphysician HMO executives or chief financial officers and directors of compensation and benefits. To a great extent, HMO medical directors had little, if any, role in this extremely important negotiating process. It was usually left to nonphysician executive, financial, or operational types. However, this can and should change in the near future.

To a significant extent, it has become apparent that there is really very little to commend one HMO or other type of health plan over another. As a result of tedious negotiating processes in the past, essentially all HMO or other alternative delivery plans have come to offer essentially the same type and range of services, choice of providers, degree of ancillary service coverage, and dependents' and out-of-plan coverage. The only factor that ultimately may have been distinguishable was the payment amount, although there was no demonstrably objective methodology for determining what this payment amount should be. Because physicians (even medical directors) had no particular expertise in financial negotiations (as compared with that of nonphysician HMO executive directors or chief operating or financial officers), they were generally excluded from these negotiations altogether.

With the advent of cost and quality competition in the HMO marketplace, this has changed dramatically. In the past, HMOs competed with other HMOs and with more traditional players primarily on the basis of price and, to a lesser extent, the type and range of services and choices of providers. Now that computerized methodologies are emerging that will permit severity-adjusted quality of care, and cost effectiveness comparisons among competing HMOs, PPOs, Blue Cross/Blue Shield, and commercial insurance plans, HMO medical directors should assume a pivotal role in this negotiation process.[2]

HMO medical directors can and should bring a specialized expertise to the negotiation process with fourth-party payers that their nonphysician executives will need. Specifically, physician executives should be able to provide objective data for negotiations with fourth-party payers concerning the HMO's clinical and cost-effectiveness performance relative to other plans in at least the following areas:

- The severity-adjusted charges and costs to HMOs generated by participating providers for specific types of patients (arranged by DRG or Major Disease Category, depending on the numbers required to demonstrate statistically significant differences among plans).

■ Improvements in these charge and cost parameters from previous contract periods as a result of provider education in cost containment.

■ The rates for severity-adjusted mortality, infection, readmission, and the like for the HMOs' participating providers arranged by DRG or Major Disease Category.

■ Improvements in these rates for the participating providers of that HMO relative to previous contract periods as a result of provider education in quality assurance.

■ Improvements in severity-adjusted inappropriate hospitalizations, invasive procedures, and intensive care unit stays from previous contracting periods and relative to comparable plans as a result of provider education and managed care enhancements.

All of the foregoing data can be generated from automated quality assessment methodologies now available. These data will be invaluable to HMO medical directors in the future as they assume their new role in the negotiation process with fourth-party payers.

The Emerging Role of the HMO Medical Director as a Purchaser in Negotiations with Hospitals and Their Medical Staffs

When wearing a purchaser hat, an HMO medical director must assume the role of a physician executive seeking the best overall depth and breadth of accessible health care services for the lowest possible cost to subscribers and the plan itself. A partial list of contractual provisions include:

■ Fiscal provisions (compensation method, degree of risk sharing, availability of equity).

■ Medical staff issues (membership requirements, recruitment, degree of risk sharing).

■ Exclusivity of the arrangement.

■ Quality assurance and utilization review (including who supplies the medical director, QA/UR personnel, or committee members).

■ Preadmission certification (whether for elective or emergency admissions, verification necessary, etc.).

■ Claims processing (billing procedures and timing).

■ Advertising (use of hospital or clinic name by the HMO, use of the HMO logo by hospital).

- Governance (including board representation and provision of administrative services).

- Data sharing (including performance profiling, confidentiality, provider charge comparisons, etc.).

- Dispute resolution alternatives (arbitration, mediation, etc.).

- Reinsurance availability.

- Indemnification for professional liability (by the hospital for medical staff members under their QA program "hold harmless" provisions).

- Termination of contract (including conditions, provisions for automatic renewal, and effect of termination).

Analysis of an HMO Medical Director's Input into the Negotiation of Specific Contractual Provisions with Physicians and Hospitals

Risk Sharing Financial Provisions

The trend is for providers to have an increasing percentage of their total compensation placed "at risk." While this has the effect of increasing their responsibilities for averting negative consequences, it often carries the opportunity for substantial rewards.

It is essential that hospitals know up front their relative clinical performance and cost-effectiveness so that they can account for these variables in arriving at an appropriate balance of risk and reward during compensation negotiations. The HMO medical director's emerging role in this new era of alternative delivery system contracting will be to assess just how well (or not so well) negotiating hospitals and physicians really do know their clinical performance and cost-effectiveness relative to their competitors. If thoroughly versed in the cost and quality assessment methodologies beginning to be used by progressive hospitals and their medical staffs, the HMO medical director should be able to make this assessment.[2]

Medical Staff Provisions

Physician credentialing is the "heart and soul" of medical staff provisions. It is absolutely essential that a hospital's credentialing practices are sound. The HMO medical director must be confident that the hospital medical staff's accrediting procedures will work to exclude the severity-adjusted low-quality and high-cost types of physicians from plan membership. Again, the HMO medical director must be intimately familiar with both the theory behind and the actual usage of the cost and quality assessment methodologies utilized by hospital medical staff credentialing committees to ensure the inclusion in the plan of only those physicians who practice both high quality and cost effective medicine. The HMO medical director should recruit those primary care physicians who come out looking "the best" based upon these clinical performance parameters and make them the chief "gatekeepers" or "value optimizers" in the plan.[3]

Utilization Review and Quality Assurance Provisions (Including Preadmission Certification)

The HMO and the hospital and its medical staff should be in tune when it comes to utilization review and quality assurance provisions, but often they are not. Clearly, their ends are in concert: the provision of high-quality care at the lowest possible cost. It is the means by which to achieve this salutary goal where the negotiation process may go awry.

As implied previously, the chances that an HMO will be able to compete effectively for fourth-party payer contracts depends on the strength of its QA and UR programs. The HMO's medical director should insist that the most vigorous, state-of-the-art cost accounting and quality assessment methodology, consistent with each participating hospital's resources and internal operations, is in place and operating as intended.

Probably the area in which HMOs have received the most "bad press" in the past few years has been preadmission certification or "prior authorization" provisions. To be effective, prior authorization must be adequately explained, accepted by physicians and plan enrollees, and not be oppressive administratively. This is particularly true for elective admissions and the performance of elective procedures.

In the area of emergency admissions, it is important for the HMO medical director to be reasonable. Good faith determinations by hospital emergency department personnel should be accepted as final by the plan, with reimbursement forthcoming. The criteria by which emergency care is delivered must be explicitly defined during the negotiation process. As a follow-up, it would be important for the medical director to communicate the HMO's criteria (in laymen's terms) to all subscribers of the plan at regular intervals.

Data Sharing Provisions

The HMO medical director should press participating hospitals for as much quality assessment, utilization management, cost accounting, and related data as possible. An increasingly common (and extremely important) point for future negotiations for HMO medical directors will concern not only which methodologies are used by participating providers, but to what extent the extra costs of a particular data assessment methodology may be shared between the HMO and providers and how this might affect other financial provisions.

Modifications in the Negotiations Process for Medical Directors in Different HMO Types

Staff Model [1]

As stated earlier in this chapter (1), in the staff model HMO, physicians are employees. As a result, these types of HMOs have the greatest potential to control physician practice patterns. During the contract negotiations process with prospective physician employees, the HMO medical director may be considerably more forceful concerning the need for compliance with protocols or care plans.

Also, because most care is usually dispensed in this type of HMO model from one or more centralized medical centers, there should not be that much discretion concerning uniform utilization of medical information systems to assess the relative quality and cost-effectiveness of health care providers and facilities. Compensation can and should be tied to quality and cost-effectiveness performance as measured by these systems. Credentialing should be uniform for all physicians and other employed health care providers. Data cost and quality determinations should be fully open to all providers and the medical director at all times in a staff model HMO.

Group Model [1]

In this model, medical groups contract with the HMO to provide care only to HMO enrollees. Because each group physician's patients are usually exclusively HMO enrollees, the HMO medical director should be able to exert almost as much control over the enforcement of quality assurance, utilization review, and credentialing systems as in the staff model HMO. Again, compensation should be tied to quality and cost-effectiveness determinations using uniform medical information systems. Data sharing among the groups to establish and refine performance profiles can and should flow freely. If to any extent physicians in a group could not serve as substitutes for physicians in another group, the HMO medical director should make sure that physician- patient confidentiality is protected through clauses in physicians' contracts.

The IPA Model [1]

The Independent Practice Association is a far looser HMO model than the staff or group versions. Participating providers in an IPA may be in either solo practice or in a group and merely agree to treat HMO patients along with the rest of their fee-for-service patients, who, very often, still constitute the bulk of their practices. The HMO contracts with the IPA, which generally has its own officers and medical directors.

In the HMO/IPA model, the HMO medical director must negotiate quality assurance, utilization management, physician credentialing, incentive compensation, and data sharing provisions through the officers of each contracting IPA. The financial strength of the HMO relative to that of the contracting IPA will determine the extent to which these items may be an integral part of the IPA's participation.

On the other hand, the HMO does contract directly with participating hospitals. For inpatient care at least, the HMO medical director can exert substantial influence on the hospital concerning the means by which the quality and the cost-effectiveness of care to enrollees is ensured.

The Network Model [1]

This model is similar to the HMO/IPA, except that the HMO contracts directly with the physician groups as solo practitioners. Accordingly, the HMO medical director should be able to exercise commensurately more bargaining clout during negotiations with the participating providers concerning compliance with the HMO's quality assurance, utilization review, physician credentialing, incentive compensation, and data sharing systems goals and the means to achieve those goals.

Summary

As purchasers, HMOs strive to ensure the highest quality care from their participating providers for each dollar spent. As providers, they also compete with other plans on the basis of the quality and cost effectiveness of their entire plans.

HMO medical directors' primary role in this process should be to optimize HMOs' competitive posture by being able to demonstrate to fourth-party payers their severity-adjusted superior quality and cost-effectiveness. An HMO medical director should be involved not only to convince fourth-party payers to contract with the HMO, but also to provide the hard data to optimize reimbursement negotiations.

As a purchaser, the HMO medical director can utilize his expertise most effectively to optimize the HMO's negotiating posture by concentrating on the following contractual issues: the determination of risk-sharing financial provisions (i.e., incentive compensation tied to quality and cost-effective performance of participating providers); the effectiveness of the quality assurance, utilization review, and physician credentialing programs of participating providers; the methodologies used to assess clinical performance data, the uses to which this data will be put, and the financial consequences flowing from any arrangements for sharing the administrative costs of these data management systems.

The HMO medical director can and should be instrumental in providing the information and the medical analysis of the data necessary to achieve the most equitable resolution of the foregoing issues consistent with the ultimate goal of improving the competitive position of the HMO through the demonstrable provision of higher quality and more cost-effective health care. These are the areas in which HMO medical directors' specific expertise should have the greatest benefit during the contract negotiation process in the days ahead.

As direct control of the HMO corporation becomes progressively greater from IPA to network to medical group to staff model, the HMO medical director can and should exercise increasingly greater bargaining clout to ensure compliance of participating providers with the HMO's various quality assurance, utilization management, physician credentialing, incentive compensation, and data management systems to help achieve the ultimate goal of making the HMO higher quality, more cost-effective, and more competitive.

References

1. *HMOs: Should You Participate.* Philadelphia: Council on Medical Practice, Pennsylvania Medical Society, 1986.

2. Couch, J. "Assessing Medical Care on the Basis of its Value." *Physician Executive* 13(4):7-11, July-Aug. 1987.

3. *Contracting With Alternative Delivery Systems.* Harrisburg: Hospital Association of Pennsylvania, 1986 pp. III-2-12.

4. Jacobs, C., and Couch, J. "Medical Care Value Purchasing and the Medical Illness Severity Grouping System--The Role of the Internist." *The Internist* 28(8):16-19,31, Sept. 1987.

Chapter 5

PHYSICIAN CONTRACTING

WITH PREFERRED

PROVIDER ORGANIZATIONS

Dale H. Cowan, MD, JD

To facilitate an understanding of contracts between physicians and Preferred Provider Organizations (PPOs), it is useful to consider first what PPOs are, their basic characteristics, and the benefits they seek to provide to the contracting parties and to those affected by the contracts.

This chapter will begin by reviewing these issues. It will then consider the contracting process and how physician contracting may vary according to the nature of the PPO sponsor. There will follow an exposition of the terms of contracts for physician services, with an analysis of their implications. Examples of terms from specific contracts will be used to illustrate the discussion. The chapter will conclude with questions physicians should ask before signing membership agreements with PPOs.

General Considerations

Definitions and Characteristics of PPOs

Preferred Provider Organizations are entities that develop, sponsor, facilitate, and/or promote contractual arrangements between health care providers (professional and/or institutional) and health care insurers or payers to provide health care services to a defined population at established fees and in accordance with an agreed-upon fee structure.

Although there is no "typical" PPO--their organization and structure vary greatly--all PPOs share some basic characteristics:

■ A designated panel of professional and institutional providers that are the "preferred" providers.

- Medical services provided on a fee-for-service basis.

- An established fee schedule that may, but need not, result in discounts from the prevailing (usual and customary) rates paid by the purchasers of care.

- A detailed program for review of utilization and claims, including some form of control mechanism.

- Flexibility in the choice of provider--no "lock-in" of the patient/consumer to specific providers.

- No formal risk-sharing arrangements by the providers, as exist in HMOs.

- Financial incentives for consumers to select the preferred option and to utilize "preferred" providers.

- An effort to pay providers within a designated time.

Benefits of PPOs

PPOs offer potential benefits to all parties that contract with them or that are affected by the contracts.

Physicians who contract with PPOs can:

- Maintain or expand their patient bases.
- Increase their proportions of private-pay patients.
- Maintain fee-for-service practices.
- Improve cash flow and reduce bad debts.
- Avoid being at financial risk.
- Obtain marketing advantages.
- Improve their relationships with hospitals.

Contracts with PPOs can enable hospitals to:

- Maintain or expand their patient bases.
- Increase the proportions of private-pay patients.
- Develop closer affiliations with their medical staffs.
- Create referral and program linkages with other institutions.
- Develop relationships with insurers and employers.
- Improve cash flow.
- Reduce financial risks.

By sponsoring or contracting with PPOs, insurers can:

- Maintain or expand their market shares.
- Offer a variety of health plans to purchasers and subscribers.
- Exercise greater control over the cost and the quality of the services that they are insuring.

- Form direct linkages with defined groups of providers.
- Compete more effectively.

Employers that contract with PPOs enhance their ability to:

- Reduce their health care costs.
- Offer attractive alternative choice of health benefits to their employees.
- Foster dialogues with providers to develop new programs and cooperate on ways to contain costs.

Patients' participation in PPOs arises from their signing subscriber agreements. The benefits of such agreements are:

- Flexibility in selecting physicians.
- No "lock-in."
- Reduced out-of-pocket expenses.
- Coverage for expanded types of services, including prevention and wellness.

It is important to keep in mind the benefits the different parties to PPO agreements hope to realize when considering the terms of contracts, because it is the terms of the contracts that will enable the different parties to achieve their respective goals and realize these benefits.

Disadvantages of PPOs

Contracting with PPOs can subject physicians to more intense accountability with respect to fees and utilization, create susceptibility to influence by employers or insurers regarding the provision and utilization of health care services and other providers, engender conflicts with hospitals over policies, pricing, and utilization, and create conflicts with other physicians.

Hospitals entering PPO contracts may experience decreased bed utilization as care is shifted from the inpatient to ambulatory or office settings, decreased income, and conflicts with medical staffs.

Insurance companies may not be able to contract with sufficient numbers of providers representing the range of services required for a credible viable program. Additionally, they remain at risk financially if the PPO performs poorly.

Employers may also be at financial risk for poor performance of PPOs. Additionally, they risk employee dissatisfaction if the services provided through the PPO are inconvenient, inadequate, or lacking in quality.

Finally, patients may find the arrangements unsatisfactory if there is restriction, real or perceived, in their choice of providers; if they must change physicians unwillingly; or if the services lack quality or are otherwise felt to be unsatisfactory.

As with the potential benefits from PPO contracts, these potential disadvantages must be kept in mind during the development and negotiation of contracts.

The Contracting Process

In the usual business setting, one party to a proposed contract commonly prepares a draft agreement for review by the other party. This draft serves as a basis for negotiation. In the case of PPOs, physician membership agreements are ordinarily prepared by the PPOs. Once the agreements are drafted, they are presented to the physicians for their review and approval. The bargaining power of physicians asked to sign PPO participation agreements varies according to whether the physicians are acting individually or as part of a large, organized group.

Individual physicians are in relatively weak positions to negotiate significant changes in the contracts presented to them. PPOs prefer to have uniform agreements with all their providers. They are particularly reluctant, if not totally unwilling, to agree to changes in key terms of the agreement, such as those pertaining to fees and utilization review, to accommodate the desires of individual physicians. Lacking the technical knowledge, the financial resources to retain knowledgeable negotiators, or the bargaining power to induce PPOs to change terms of proposed agreements, individual physicians usually have little choice but to accept or reject the agreements that are presented to them.

In contrast, physicians who are part of an organized group are in a much better position to negotiate the terms of agreements. Groups have greater financial resources to retain able negotiators. Additionally, the prospect of enlisting an entire panel of physicians representing the spectrum of medical specialties with a single set of negotiations creates a strong incentive for PPOs to modify contract language to accommodate the wishes of the physicians.

Physician bargaining power also varies according to the nature of the entity sponsoring the PPO. PPOs are sponsored by physicians, hospitals, physician-hospital joint ventures, insurance companies, employers, third-party administrators, and entrepreneurs. PPOs sponsored by provider groups usually have physicians participate in the process of drafting the physician membership agreement. The participating physicians can be expected to be sensitive to the interests and concerns of their colleagues. The terms of agreements from provider-sponsored PPOs are more likely, therefore, to strike a balance between the needs and interests of the PPOs and those of the physicians.

PPOs sponsored by nonprovider entities may be expected to be less interested than provider-sponsored PPOs in drafting terms of physician participation agreements that are sensitive to the interests and concerns of physicians. Although precise data are lacking, it can be assumed that the input of physicians in the development of physician participation agreements by nonprovider-sponsored PPOs is limited, if it exists at all. Consequently, the need for physicians to appraise the terms of PPO participation agreements and understand the implications of specific terms, while always present, is greater in the case of contracts submitted by nonprovider-sponsored PPOs as compared to those submitted by provider-sponsored PPOs.

The Physician Participation Agreement

The physician contract or membership participation agreement consists of two forms. One is an application for membership on the physician panel of the PPO--i.e., the application to become a "preferred" provider. The other is the agreement itself. The latter sets out the rights, duties, and responsibilities of the PPO and the physicians.

The Application Form

There are two general types of application forms. One is used by PPOs that have a policy of accepting all applicants as members of the provider panel. It generally requests basic demographic information:

- Name

- Office address and phone number

- Home address and phone number

- Night/weekend phone number

- Medical license number and date of last renewal

- Type of practice, including specialty and/or subspecialty

- Board certification

- Social Security and federal ID numbers

- Professional liability coverage, including name of carrier and amount of coverage

- Hospitals where applicant has privileges and class of privilege

- Statement warranting accuracy of the information provided.

The information provided, except for personal information such as home address and telephone numbers, may be used by the PPO in marketing brochures and other marketing activities. It also allows the PPO to certify that its panel of physicians is able to provide a broad range of medical services. The information is not intended to serve as a basis for credentialing.

The second type of application is lengthier and is intended to serve a credentialing function. It enables the PPO to determine whether or not to grant the applicant membership on the panel of preferred providers. This application will request, in addition to the items listed above, information regarding the applicant's:

- Education and training

- Professional activities undertaken since completion of training

- Professional honors

- Society memberships

- Faculty positions

- Publications

- Loss, suspension, or reduction of privileges, with reasons

- Loss or suspension of licensure, with reasons

- Malpractice actions and/or loss of professional liability coverage

- Convictions for felonies and loss of narcotics license

- Current fee schedules

- Utilization profiles.

Applicants may be requested to supply the names of individuals who can vouch for their professional competence and personal character. The information that is requested attempts to provide the selection committee of the PPO with data regarding each applicant's economic performance and quality of medical care.

The Contract

PPO contracts for physician services are lengthy and complex. The presence of specific provisions and the manner in which the terms are worded vary greatly. Because there is no perfect agreement, the following discussion will analyze the terms that are most commonly found (or should be) in contracts. Examples of representative terms from contracts will be provided to highlight the discussion.

The Opening Paragraph

The opening paragraph of the contract should clearly identify the parties to the agreement. A representative opening paragraph might be:

This agreement is made this _____ day of _____, 198__, by and between _____ (full name of PPO) and_____(Practitioner).

It is important that all entities responsible for operating the PPO be identified, particularly if the PPO is sponsored by or is part of a national organization. Where more then one entity is involved on the PPO side, the contracting physician needs to know the roles and obligations of each and which entity has the ultimate responsibility for executing the PPO's obligations.

The "Recitals"

The opening paragraph is commonly followed by a "Recitals" section, each statement of which starts with the word "Whereas." The statements identify the sponsor and operator of the PPO, state that the physician is licensed to practice medicine in the state, express in general terms the purpose of the contractual arrangement, and indicate the desire of the parties that the physician be a member of the provider panel of the PPO.

Definitions

A good agreement provides concise definitions of all special terms that are used in it. The purpose of the definitions is to minimize confusion or ambiguity in the interpretation of specific terms of the agreement. Terms for which definitions should be provided include:

- Alternate provider
- Covered services
- Eligible persons
- Health service provider
- Hospital provider
- Managed care plan
- Panel of providers
- Participating provider
- Peer review panel
- Purchaser
- Purchaser agreement
- Physician provider

Definitions of the elements of the utilization review (UR) program ordinarily are provided in the section that describes UR. Definitions of some terms may require further elaboration in the contract. For example, one contract defines "Covered Services" as the health care services provided pursuant to a purchaser agreement. Without knowing the terms of the purchaser agreement, the physician has no way of knowing which services are covered and which are not covered for purposes of payment and utilization review.

Relationship Between the Parties

This term specifies that the physician is and remains an independent contractor. The contract does not create an employment relationship between the PPO and the physician.

Physicians' Warranties

Each contract has a section in which the physician warrants certain facts. A representative warranty clause reads as follows:

Physician warrants and represents that he/she is licensed to practice his/her specialty in this state and that the statements set forth herein and in the application for membership, attached hereto, are true and may be relied upon by PPO, and will continue to be true thoughout the term of this Agreement and any renewal hereof unless the physician notifies PPO in writing that any such statements are no longer true.

Physicians' Service and Obligations

Although the specific obligations of the physicians may vary from one agreement to another, all agreements contain provisions regarding:

- Adherence to the rules and regulations of the PPO.

- Willingness to provide services to subscribers of plans that contract with the PPO.

- Participation in utilization review activities.

- Acceptance of the PPO payment schedule.

- Willingness to refer patients who are insured under a PPO service agreement to other preferred providers.

Adherence to policies and procedures

An example of a provision regarding adherence to policies and procedures is:

Physician agrees to comply with and be bound by the rules, regulations, and policies of PPO as they now exist and that may hereafter be adopted or amended from time to time.

Before agreeing to such a provision, it is advisable for physicians to have copies of the rules, regulations, and policies of the PPO, because the physicians will be required to adhere to them under the contract. It is unwise for physicians to agree to be bound by new terms and conditions without having an opportunity to review them in advance of their adoption. That is, it is not advisable for physicians to sign agreements the terms of which may be amended or revised unilaterally by the PPO. Rather, there should be provisions allowing physicians to review proposed changes in terms and accept or reject them without risking termination of the entire agreement. Additionally, there should be provisions that allow physicians to propose amendments or new terms for the agreement.

Willingness to provide services to subscribers

There are several formulations that express the willingness of the physician to provide services to subscribers (patients) of the plans that contract with the PPO. Examples of contract language are:

Example 1:

Physician agrees to perform all medical and health care services the physician is qualified to perform for individual patients as are included within contractual arrangements by and between PPO and subscribers. Physician shall be responsible for maintaining a professional relationship with individual patients, and no provision of this agreement has or is intended to have the effect of infringing upon the physician's relationship with said individual patients.

Example 2:

Physician shall make available covered physician's services to PPO-covered persons on the same basis as such services are made available to other patients. Physician shall be solely responsible for the qualtiy of services rendered PPO-covered persons. Physician shall not deny provision of covered physician services to any PPO-covered person by virtue of the individual's covered status under this agreement.

Example 3:

Physician shall provide covered services to covered persons in accordance with the standards and procedures applicable to physicians or their patients.

The key feature of these terms is that the physician will adhere to the same standards of care in treating patients who are subscribers of PPO plans as are ordinarily and customarily performed by physicians practicing in that specialty. On its face, the terms merely restate the fundamental legal and fiduciary responsibilities all physicians assume upon establishing a physician- patient relationship with a particular patient.

A problem with these terms arises when other terms in the contract appear to limit the physician's clinical decision making. Conflicts may arise between the physician adhering to the prevailing standards of care and complying with a PPO's UR program or compensation plan.

Participation in utilization review activites

Utilization review activities are the most important aspect of a PPO's cost containment and quality review functions. An effective program for utilization review is essential for PPOs' continued viability. Representative language regarding participation in utilization review activities follows:

Example 1:

Physician shall participate in and actively cooperate with the PPO utilization review program, including, but not limited to, initiating certain procedures relating to preadmission certification, emergency admission certification, and extension of hospital stays. Such certification is required for care rendered at acute and extended care facilities and for home health care programs, hospice programs, private duty nursing, and certain other programs. The UR program includes procedures for physician review and appeals. Failure of physician to comply with UR policies and procedures may result in reduced reimbursement by payer for covered services rendered to covered persons or in termination of this Agreement.

Physician acknowledges that he/she has an independent responsibility to provide medical care to covered persons and that any action by PPO or payer, pursuant to the UR program and/or the general administration of the PPO program, in no way absolves the physician of the responsibility to provide appropriate medical care to covered persons.

Example 2:

Physician agrees that he/she shall accept PPO's quality review and utilization management programs set out in Exhibit__ hereto and incorporated herein by this reference as from time-to-time amended, willingly participate in and observe the protocols of the UR program, and be bound by the decisions resulting therefrom.

Example 3:

Physician agrees to abide by and take responsibility for the implementation of PPO contract terms regarding preadmission review, customized care, mandatory second surgical opinions, and particpation in alternative treatment planning and case management designed to facilitate more cost-effective care.

Example 4:

Physician shall make available covered physician services to PPO-covered persons on the same basis as such services are made available to other patients. Physician shall be solely responsible for the quality of services rendered PPO-

covered persons. Physician shall not deny provision of covered physician services to any PPO-covered person by virtue of the individual's covered status under this Agreement.

It is essential that physicians understand the consequences of these terms. The standard of care owed to patients by physicians remains the same regardless of any constraints placed on physicians by the contract's utilization review procedures. This is clearly set out in the two paragraphs in the first example shown above. The concept was also articulated by the California Court of Appeals in *Wickline v. State of California*, in which the court stated:

"As to the principal issue before this court, i.e., who bears responsibility for allowing a patient to be discharged from the hospital, her treating physician's or the health care payer, each side's medical expert witnesses agreed that, in accordance with the standards of medical practice... it (is) for the patient's treating physician to decide the course of treatment that (is) medically necessary to treat the ailment.

"Third-party payers of health care services can be held legally accountable when medically inappropriate decisions result from defects in the design or implementation of cost containment mechanisms, as, for example, when appeals made on a patient's behalf for medical or hospital care are arbitrarily ignored or unreasonably disregarded or overridden. *However, the physician who complies without protest with the limitations imposed by a third-party payer, when his medical judgment dictates otherwise, cannot avoid his ultimate responsibility for his patient's care.* He cannot point to the health payer as the liability scapegoat when the consequences of his own determinative medical decisions go sour." (Emphasis added).

Because physician liability for care exists independently of any restrictions arising from the application of the utilization review plan, it is essential that the physician review and understand all aspects of the plan. Commonly, as indicated by the language in the second example shown above, the utilization review plan is provided in an appendix or exhibit attached to the contract. The descriptions of the plans should be available for review and should be affixed to the contract. It is unwise for physicians to sign agreements promising to adhere to conditions the details of which are not know to them.

The utilization review plan ordinarily includes several features:

■ The components of the plan, such as preadmission certification, postadmission review, concurrent utilization, and retrospective review.

■ The identity of the reviewers.

■ The criteria used for review.

■ Procedures for appealing from denials.

Acceptance of the PPO payment schedule

The description of the components of the utilization review plan should indicate the criteria according to which decisions are made. The description should also indicate whether the PPO is conducting the utilization review or whether reviews are contracted to an outside group; whether denials can be issued by any reviewer or only by a physician with the same specialty as the physician facing the denial; whether appeals can be generated by the patient, the physician, or both; and whether denial of medical necessity in retrospective reviews results in no payment for care already provided.

The second major feature of programs offered to purchasers by PPOs is a schedule of benefits that includes a fee structure designed to limit the costs to be paid by the purchasers and their subscriber employees. To tie physicians to the benefit plan, the membership agreement contains clauses that require physician compliance with the benefits programs. Operative terms may be brief:

Physician accepts as full payment for the covered services provided to eligible persons pursuant to purchaser agreements accepted by the physician the fee set out in Exhibit__ hereto.

A compensation clause of this type should be accompanied by a reasonably detailed schedule of payments, including the presence and amount, if any, of deductibles and copayments. An additional clause may specify that neither the PPO nor the subscriber shall have any liability to the physician for any payment with respect to charges for covered services that are in excess of the fee schedule.

Alternatively, the operative terms may be lengthy and complex:

PPO shall arrange for physician to be compensated by payer for covered services rendered to covered persons according to the reimbursement methodology specified in Exhibit___. Physician shall only be entitled to bill and collect from covered persons any applicable copayments, coinsurance amounts, and deductibles or amounts for noncovered services. PPO shall arrange for payer to pay physician's claims for covered services when such claims are accurate, complete, and in the form designated in section___ of this agreement within 30 days of receipt, subject to applicable subrogation and coordination of benefits rules. Payer shall be entitled to reimbursement from physician of any amount paid pursuant to any assignment of benefits that is subsequently contested and found to be deficient.

Physician shall cooperate with payer in its claims payment administration, including, but not limited to, its coordination of benefits, verification of coverage, and record keeping procedures.

A somewhat different formulation of these terms is:

The total amount for which physician will be compensated for covered physician services shall be equal to physician's normal charge or PPO's maximum allowable fee. If the physician's normal charge exceeds PPO's maximum allowable fee, the physician agrees not to bill PPO-covered person the difference.

The PPO shall pay physician for covered physician services the amount noted in Section___ above less any amount payable therefore by the PPO-covered person under the applicable group health plan.

As with the briefer language cited above, these terms refer to separate schedules, exhibits, or attachments for the complete details of the compensation program. An important difference exists, however, in the terms set out immediately above. One contract obligates the PPO to pay the physician. The other states that the PPO will *arrange* for payment but has no responsibility for providing payment. Contracts providing for the latter mechanism should include terms whereby the PPO assures the physician that PPO- purchaser contracts will specify that the purchaser is to pay the physician directly. Additionally, the physician agreement should indicate that physicians can bill patients directly for payments for covered services for which purchasers refuse or fail to pay. Although the PPO may object to such a clause, it provides some protection for physicians entering into agreements with PPOs that are acting as third-party intermediaries in the payment process and not as payers.

Some PPOs have a uniform schedule of benefits, including covered services, copayments, and deductibles. This schedule is used in each purchaser agreement. Physicians contracting with PPOs with a single benefit schedule should be readily able to assess the potential effect of the contract on their revenues and should be able to implement the necessary collection procedures to comply with the schedule.

Other PPOs write separate benefits schedules for each purchaser. Physicians contracting with PPOs that adopt this approach should include in the membership agreements a term that requires the PPO to send to each physician a schedule of benefits, including the list of covered services and the amount of deductibles and coinsurance. This is the only way the physicians have to know whom to bill and for which services.

Additional terms in the section on compensation should indicate the procedures for submitting claims, to whom claims should be sent, the person or entity responsible for approving claims, and the mechanism for getting paid if a subscriber agreement is terminated without the knowledge of the physician before services are provided.

Willingness to refer covered persons to other preferred providers

PPOs depend for their effectiveness on the fact that services to subscribers will be provided by individuals and institutions that have entered into participating agreements with them and have consequently become "preferred" providers. Membership agreements generally include terms that restrict referrals to other panel members. Representative language providing for preferential referral to other panel members states:

Physician shall use his/her best efforts to refer, when medically necessary, PPO-covered persons to other physicians participating in the PPO. Physician is to use his/her efforts to admit, when medically necessary, PPO-covered persons to hospitals participating in the PPO.

Physician shall utilize PPO hospitals and other PPO preferred providers whenever medically appropriate when arranging for additional services required for covered persons.

An administrative consequence of these terms is that the physician must be provided with updated rosters of participating physicians and institutions. A consequence that affects the quality of care and a physician's responsibility for treating a PPO patient like every other patient, using a single standard of care, arises if other participating physicians in specific subspecialties or in institutions offering specific services are not deemed to be as qualified or capable of rendering a particular service as one who is not a panel member. This restriction has the potential of creating a conflict for physicians between adhering to the terms of the contract and upholding their fiduciary duty to their patients.

In order to address this situation, it is suggested that the agreement provide a mechanism for physicians to refer patients to nonpanel providers if, in their medical judgment, it is appropriate to do so. Such a referral can be made subject to a timely prospective review and approval to protect the PPO from excess or inappropriate referrals.

Professional Liability Insurance

PPOs generally require, as a condition of membership on the provider panel, that the physician carry professional liability coverage. Contracts vary on whether an amount of coverage is specified. Often the controlling factor is the amount of coverage physicians must have as a condition of membership on the medical staffs of individual hospitals. Increasingly, hospitals' liability insurers are requiring, as a condition of hospital liability coverage, that the governing body of the hospital require each physician to maintain a specified level of coverage.

The contract term may require the physician to supply the PPO with proof of coverage and with notice if there is any adverse change in coverage.

Liability/Indemnification

All physician malpractice liability policies prohibit or do not cover liability assumed by virtue of contract. The physician membership agreement should therefore *not* contain any "hold harmless" clauses or other language by which physicians assume or acquire any liability for acts or omissions of the PPO or its owners, officers, managers, employees, or contractees. It is best if the contract clearly states that neither the PPO nor the physician, nor any of their respective agents or employees, shall be liable for any act or omission of the other party.

Physicians signing contracts with "hold harmless" clauses risk, at the least, being personally liable for any damages that are attributed to them as a consequence of an act or omission of the PPO or, more likely, having their malpractice liability policy nullified and terminated.

Notice of Malpractice and Disciplinary Proceedings

As part of their effort to maintain a panel of providers who have good reputations for practicing high-quality medicine, PPOs commonly want to be notified of any malpractice action brought against a physician or of any disciplinary proceeding that might affect the physician's licensure, medical staff privileges, or ability to practice.

An example of such a term is:

Physician shall notify PPO within five (5) calendar days of the occurrence of any of the following:

--any action taken to restrict, suspend, or revoke a physician's license to practice medicine; or

--any action taken to restrict, suspend, or revoke a physician's medical staff privileges; or

--any suit brought aginst physician for malpractice and the final disposition of such action; or

--failure to maintain physician's professional liability insurance in accordance with this agreement; or

--any other situation that might materially affect physician's ability to carry out his/her duties and obligations under this agreement.

The language in this example is subject to varying interpretations. The words "any action taken" in the first two clauses could refer to final actions. Alternatively, they could refer to the initial step in taking an action without reference to the outcome. The latter would be overreaching, because actions are not infrequently initiated that do not result in any change in licensure or privileges. To avoid such ambiguity, it is best to indicate at what point in the course of the proceedings actions being taken that affect licensure or privileges should be reported.

The request to report any suit brought against a physician is also overly broad. The explosion in malpractice litigation makes it inevitable that a significant number of physicians will have malpractice actions brought against them. Because more than 80 percent of such actions are won by the defendant physicians, it is difficult to see how reporting all of the actions would safeguard or promote the interests of the PPOs.

In contrast, PPOs would appear to have a legitimate interest in knowing of settlements or decisions adverse to physicians, because they could affect their operations.

Medical Records

PPOs often desire that the medical records of subscribers be maintained for a specified period and be available to them for inspection. A representative clause reads:

Physician shall maintain medical records of covered persons and preserve them for the longer of five years or such a period as is required by applicable law, regulations, and practices. Such medical records shall be treated as confidential so as to comply with all state and federal laws and regulations regarding the confidentiality of patient records. Subject to such confidentiality requirements, physician shall make such records reasonably available to PPO during the term of this agreement and as may be reasonably requested following termination.

If the term indicates that duplicate copies of the medical records be made available to the PPO, the party responsible for paying for duplicating the records should be specified. Duplication of medical records is time-consuming and expensive. Because PPOs will be using the records for administrative purposes and will generate revenues to pay for administrative expenses, it is appropriate that the duplicating costs be borne by the PPOs. In this regard, it is noteworthy that the federal courts have ruled that Medicare must pay the costs of duplicating medical records requested for peer review purposes.

Confidentiality

Related to the issue of medical records is confidentiality. The agreement should include a statement such as the following:

PPO and the physician, their officers, directors, employees, and agents shall hold confidential information in the strictest confidence as fiduciaries and shall not, voluntarily or involuntarily, sell, transfer, publish, disclose, display, or otherwise make available to others any portion of the confidential information or related materials without the express written consent of the other party. PPO and the physician shall use their best efforts to protect the confidential information consistent with the manner in which they protect their most confidential business information.

Dispute Resolution, Appeals, and Arbitration

Physician membership agreements should contain dispute resolution procedures in order to maintain smooth working relationships between physicians and the PPO. Decisions most likely to be the source of disputes are those relating to utilization review, payment, and termination. The processes for appealing adverse decisions and resolving disputes should be clearly delineated. For example, the bases for bringing the appeals, the membership of the hearing committee, and the rules governing introduction of evidence should be set out. A specific requirement should prohibit any individual who made or participated in an adverse decision from serving on the hearing board.

Similarly, in order to avoid lawsuits, there should be provisions for arbitration in order to settle disputes not resolved through the appeals procedures. The terms should indicate the processes for arbitration and state how the costs should be apportioned.

Termination

All contracts for personal services state the duration of the agreement and the conditions for terminating the relationship between the parties. A representative clause in one contract states:

The term of this agreement shall be one (1) year, beginning _____ and ending at midnight on _____, and shall be automatically renewed for one (1) year periods unless either party gives the other party sixty (60) days written notice of its intent not to renew. However, at any time during the term hereof, either physician or PPO may unilaterally terminate this agreement without cause by giving the other party at least sixty days written notice.

Contracts may provide for automatic termination if a physician's medical staff privileges are denied or license is lost or suspended, if he or she fails to maintain professional liability insurance, or if the PPO becomes insolvent or bankrupt. Sections dealing with termination should specify the rights and oligations of the parties after termination. For example:

Following the effective date of termination, this agreement shall be of no further force or effect, except that each party shall remain liable for any obligations or liabilities arising from activities carried on by it hereunder prior to the effective date of termination of this agreement.

Physicians must recognize they have ongoing fiduciary duties to their patients after termination. They may nonetheless be required to arrange for an orderly transfer of patients to other physicians.

Membership Roster and Marketing

It is common for contracts to request that physicians allow their names, addresses, business phone numbers, and types of practice to be listed on membership rosters and used in PPO marketing brochures and activities. Where they exist, such provisions should indicate that the list will be revised at regular intervals so physicians will no longer be listed on the roster of PPOs from which they have disassociated.

Miscellaneous Provisions

Physician membership agreements commonly have several miscellaneous provisions pertaining to:

- Assignment
- Severability
- Entire agreement
- Notice
- Governing law.

These terms are standard or "boilerplate" and require no special comment.

Nonexclusivity

In order to minimize the risk of antitrust liability, PPO agreements should not require that physicians contract only with a particular PPO. Instead, they should state explicity that the agreement is not exclusive and either party is free to contract with any other party.

CONTRACT ANALYSIS

It was previously observed that physicians asked to sign PPO membership agreements generally have little or no input in the drafting of the agreement. It is not surprising, therefore, that agreements drafted by one party, or more precisely, counsel for the PPO, contain terms and provisions that are more sensitive to or promote the interests of the PPO over those of the physicians. It is helpful, therefore, in reviewing proposed agreements for physicians to have in mind a series of questions regarding the contract terms. By insisting on satisfactory answers to the questions below, physicians can more effectively safeguard their interests and those of their patients.

1. Are all parties to the contract clearly identified by name?

2. What is the PPO's track record in other areas with respect to marketing, paying claims, and relating to physicians?

3. Does the contract permit unilateral changes in terms and conditions without prior notice to or assent of the physician?

4. What obligations are imposed on the physician?

5. Must the physician abide by unspecified medical policies? Does the contract refer to rules and regulations or incorporate by reference other documents or agreements not seen by the physician?

6. What restrictions are there on medical practice with respect to using contract physicians, hospitals, laboratories, and other facilities? Can any services be utilized that are outside the plan? If so, under what conditions?

7. How will physicians be paid for their services? Is there a fee schedule?

8. Is payment to physicians subject to a withhold? If so, can the percentage be changed unilaterally without prior notice to and/or assent of the physician? What happens to monies that are withheld?

9. Are there provisions for reviewing and revising the fee schedule periodcially and for introducing fees for new services?

10. Who has the responsibility for paying claims? The PPO? The subscribers? If the latter, what is the role of the PPO in facilitating or ensuring that claims are paid?

11. What are the details of the utilization review plan? Does it include preadmission certification? Postadmission and concurrent review? Retrospective review and denials?

12. Who undertakes utilization review? Who is authorized to issue denials of either preadmission certification or upon retrospective review?

13. What is the source of standards and criteria for making UR determinations?

14. What provisions are there for appealing decisions and resolving conflicts regarding utilization review and payment of claims? Are the procedures set out in the Agreement?

15. Can physicians bill for services rendered that are later denied upon retrospective review?

16. Under what circumstances can either party terminate the agreement?

17. Are there provisions for resolving disputes or contesting adverse decisions related to attempts to terminate the agreement or arising from interpretation of the agreement? What are the procedures for resolving disputes?

18. Is there any increase in personal professional liability?

19. Is there a "hold harmless" clause?

20. Is there an exclusivity clause?

21. Are there provisions for paying physicians for services rendered after subscriber contracts are terminated?

22. At what point or under what circumstances must physicians notify the PPO of any disciplinary or malpractice actions?

23. What provisions are there for maintaining confidentiality of patient records?

More complete information on analyzing contracts may be found in *Physician's Contracting Handbook*, published by the California Medical Association, and in *A Physician's Guide to Preferred Provider Organizations*, published by the American Medical Association.

Index